ARMY LIFE IN THE '90S

London · New York · Sydney · Toronto

ARMY LIFE IN THE '90S

PHILIP WARNER

COUNTRY LIFE

Published for Country Life Books by
The Hamlyn Publishing Group Limited
London·New York·Sydney·Toronto
Astronaut House, Feltham, Middlesex, England
© Copyright The Hamlyn Publishing Group Limited 1975

ISBN 0 600 30234 2

Printed by Butler & Tanner Limited, Frome and London

CONTENTS

FOREWORD

On 20 December 1895 Hudson & Keans and George Newnes Ltd. began publishing a fortnightly journal, *Navy and Army Illustrated*. It was described as 'A magazine descriptive and illustrative of everyday life in the defensive services of the British Empire', and was edited by Commander Charles Robinson, R.N.

Service life, as seen through the pages of *Navy and Army Illustrated*, is clearly something which belongs not only to a different century but also to an entirely different method of thought. Some of the illustrations and articles are stereotyped and pompous but undoubtedly they represent popular conceptions; at the same time there is much in those pages which is not unfamiliar to the serviceman of today.

Here we have the Army as presented at the end of the nineteenth century. It is all very dignified, enthusiastic and naïve, but it is also wholesome and kind. Perhaps we are wiser in our new, realistic approach, but one doubts if we are the better for it, still less happier.

Where it has been possible, I have retained the original picture captions, both for the information they contain and for the insight they give into the way the Victorians saw themselves; in some cases I have added my own comments.

Philip Warner

INTRODUCTION

In 1895, as everybody in Britain knew (or should have known), the British Army was the best in the world. This view had been formed over three centuries and was the natural consequence of Marlborough's victories in the eighteenth century, Wellington's in the nineteenth, and a host of other large and small engagements which had mostly been brought to a satisfactory conclusion during the period. It was, indeed, a very good and versatile army and the armies of other countries had every reason to respect it, though that did not prevent them from occasionally trying their luck.

A similar view of their own soldiers was doubtless held by many other countries, though possibly with less reason. The British Army in 1895 had several remarkable assets: It had vast experience; its origins went back to the Civil War and its aftermath; the eighteen years between 1642 and 1660 taught Englishmen what was needed to create a winning army. Even so it suffered subsequent setbacks. Sometimes it was badly beaten—though never disgraced. Eventually it was to prove as capable in the bitter cold of Canada as in the enervating heat of India, and from the Caribbean to China, and all in spite of appalling food, squalid accommodation, and brutal discipline. Its victories were hailed with pleasure by people who had never heard of, let alone seen, the remote and rugged places in which they were won. We were proud of our army—but as Kipling did not fail to point out—only when it was far away and winning victories; soldiers at home were a very different story.

The attitude was not entirely unreasonable in the circumstances. Soldiers 'joined up' for a number of reasons and often had records of petty crime. Some were the products of the 'Press Gang', for that recruiting procedure was not exclusive to the Navy. The officers were a mixed bag too, though in a different way. Many were fervently devoted to their troops— though not to the extent of doing much for their welfare; others were as selfish as Lord Cardigan, who campaigned in the Crimea from the comfort of his yacht. However, incompetent or

not, selfish or not, all seemed to have qualities of leadership, particularly that supreme disdain for personal safety that makes an officer loved and respected however appalling his mental deficiencies.

In 1871 the Cardwell Reforms had abolished the purchase of commissions. In the early days, when the holder of a commission fed, clothed, armed and trained his troops, the system had had some merit; but by the mid-nineteenth century it had long ceased to do so. Long service was abolished and in the ranks men served six years with the colours and six with the reserve. Equally progressive was the linking of all the regular line regiments in pairs so that one could be at home while the other was abroad. ('Line' regiments were those not assigned to special duties as were the Foot Guards, Household Cavalry and specialist corps.) In 1881 linked line regiments became the same regiment as a result of the Childers Reforms. Originally they had been distinguished by numbers; but now, for example, 28 and 61 made the Gloucestershire regiment—regiments took their title from the district in which their recruiting and training depot was situated. Soon the Militia became the 3rd battalion, and the Volunteers made the nucleus of a 4th. The Territorial affiliation was a brilliant success, although at Isandhlwana, in the Zulu War of 1879, the 24th (later the South Wales Borderers) had fought literally to the last round and the last man, as had the 66th (later the Royal Berkshires) at Maiwand in the Afghan War. However, in general, morale is more easily raised by a county name—or even a nickname—than a number.

Regimental organization differed according to the arm of the service but basically the pattern was the same. The C.O. (the commanding officer) was the pinnacle, and invariably of great importance, but the driving force of the unit was the adjutant and the regimental sergeant major. The adjutant was responsible for general discipline; whether a major or a captain he wielded considerable power by virtue of his appointment; the R.S.M. was in many people's opinion (including, of course, his own) the linchpin of the regiment. Usually—this is a very basic outline—there were four companies, each commanded by a major or captain. Each had a company sergeant major, two or three sergeants, corporals, two lance-corporals and a quota of private soldiers whose lives were conducted entirely in public.

The organization of a regiment, so puzzling to those who have never served in one—and not always apparent to those who have—may be compared to that of a normal business. The company chairman is the equivalent of the commanding officer (the C.O.), the managing director is the adjutant, the divisional managers are the company commanders (there were four to a regiment at this time); the deputy managers and foremen are the sergeant majors and sergeants, the charge hands are corporals, and the skilled and unskilled workers are privates.
Just as every true British citizen knew that ours was the best army in the world, so every soldier knew that his own regiment was the best in that army. This was a heartfelt conviction, but it did not prevent him voicing grievances among his contemporaries. But let anyone else dare to criticize the unit, or any officer or man in it, and a fight was in progress before any of the bystanders had realized what was happening.

The inner councils of the War Office did not escape his censure if he felt that other regiments were being treated with unfair discrimination. 'Fancy sending them instead of us' he would ask an indifferent audience, 'are they trying to lose the . . . war?'. When in the Sudan campaign of 1898 the Grenadier Guards, the Northumberland Fusiliers, the Rifle Brigade, the Lancashire Fusiliers and the 21st Lancers were sent up the line in the closing stages of a campaign which other regiments felt they had already won, there was considerable comment from all ranks. It was suggested that a couple of fashionable regiments had been put in at the last minute so that they could qualify for a medal ribbon they had done little to win. (Soldiers cynically describe campaign ribbons as 'luggage labels'.) In the event, the wisdom of sending the second brigade was appreciated.

An irritating characteristic of fashionable regiments was that they not only reeked of aristocracy (Captain the Hon This and Major the Earl of That) and were thus colourful, but were also so superbly good in action that they caught the public's admiration to a far greater degree than worthy but probably equally capable line regiments.

There is not a single regiment in the British army which has not at some time or other acquitted itself with almost incredibly nonchalant courage. One thinks of the Fusiliers at Albuhera, of the South Wales Borderers at Isandhlwana and Rorke's Drift, of the 2nd Devons at Bois des Buttes, of the Berkshires at Maiwand—the list could go on for a long time, and these were by no means isolated acts in the history of these regiments. There is also an impressive roll of feats performed by units which the general public imagines to be employed in some safe administrative or service task: signallers, pioneers, storemen or transport drivers. These too have behaved with amazing courage and endurance when the occasion demanded.

It is, however, a normal human reaction to be amused when a distinguished colleague comes a cropper, particularly if that colleague has been somewhat aloof and haughty. Men do not wish to see their fellows killed or injured, but there are plenty of units which other soldiers would like to see humbled a little. The Army is very proud of the Guards regiments, but a Guards officer slipping on a banana skin would be regarded as a highly satisfactory sight by members of other units. In the 1890s the military virtues of the Guards were widely appreciated, but the fact that Queen Victoria so obviously doted on them was a major irritant. At this time, and for a long time afterwards, it was felt that the Guards received the most coveted postings, such as Cairo, and there was an embittered army saying, 'It's as scarce as guardsmen's sweat in India'. What was not generally realized was that in the nineteenth century the Guards had paid more attention to the welfare of their soldiers than most other units.

In all regiments there was a considerable gap between officers and other ranks. Up till the 1960s, when the Army Public Relations Directorate began to look into such matters, the personnel of the army consisted of officers and 'other ranks'. The 'other ranks' may have included such powerful figures as sergeant-majors (warrant officers) or sergeants and corporals (non-commissioned officers) but they were branded socially as 'other ranks'. The complete dismissal of a large proportion of the Army as 'other ranks' ended when the Higher Command stated that the term would cease to be used and the word 'soldier' substituted.

However, in the 1890s, the humblest 'other rank' serving in India or some other overseas station suddenly found himself a privileged person. Native servants would sweep out his barrack room, wash his clothes, and even shave him in bed before parade. The experience of being a temporary aristocrat had a variety of effects, not all pleasing.

Back in the United Kingdom the soldier found himself regarded as a potential nuisance. Often it was justified. 'A feed, five pints, and a fight' was regarded by many as a very satisfactory programme for Saturday night, and even to this day a group of soldiers is not always welcome in a public house. Some publicans in the 1890s decided that all soldiers were liable to be drunken and quarrelsome and refused to serve any. It was felt that soldiers should be winning wars overseas, not getting drunk at home. For the soldier with little enough to spend, nowhere to go, and with little idea of how to pass the time, it was all rather embittering, as Kipling pointed out:

I went into a public-'ouse to get a pint o' beer
The publican 'e up and sez 'We serve no redcoats here'
The girls be'ind the bar they giggled fit to die
I outs into the street again and to myself sez I:
O it's Tommy this, an' Tommy that, an' Tommy go away'
But it's 'Thank-you, Mister Atkins' when the band begins to play
The band begins to play, my boys, the band begins to play
O it's Thank you, Mr Atkins, when the band begins to play.

Then it's Tommy this and Tommy that, an' 'Tommy, how's your soul?'
But it's 'Thin red line of 'eroes' when the drums begin to roll—
The drums begin to roll, my boys, the drums begin to roll
O it's 'Thin red line of 'eroes', when the drums begin to roll.

The term 'Tommy Atkins', used widely up till World War II, originated as a fictitious name used in a War Office instruction in the early nineteenth century. It has no connection with Tommy guns, which were Thompson sub-machine-guns.

In the 1890s, cavalry prestige was as high as it had ever been, which is saying a lot. The charge of the 21st Lancers at Omdurman was exactly what the nation expected of its cavalry. The Greys had distinguished themselves at Waterloo, many other units forming the heavy and the light brigades had achieved fame in the Crimea, and the idea of any other nation being able to produce regiments of similar quality was clearly unrealistic as well as being unpatriotic. Inside the army there were a few disrespectful stories circulating. One commanding officer was said to have written on an annual report, 'I would not advocate breeding from this officer', and another, 'This man's troopers would follow him anywhere, but only out of curiosity'. They were also referred to slightingly as 'donkey wallopers'.

The cavalry rode over it all. Their future would not be an easy one. There would be barbed wire and machine-guns and mechanization. They survived it, and today, although equipped with tanks and armoured cars instead of horses, they preserve, in astonishing fashion, most of their former glamour and panache.

In 1895 the Army's record was good but not perfect. Canada and New Zealand had been 'settled' twenty-five years before. People felt we had made rather a mess of it in the First Boer War of 1881, thanks to the politicians, and that would have to be put right sometime. Burma was calm but the North West frontier of India was very turbulent. West Africa looked unstable, and here—as elsewhere—our interests clashed with the French. The Entente Cordiale was still years away. Another minor blot on the military escutcheon was the Sudan, where Gordon had been murdered by the Dervishes in 1885 before our relief expedition had reached him. There were, however, signs that the Government was now belatedly going to teach the Dervishes their manners.

Not that many soldiers knew what they were supposed to be fighting for. They knew that when they got there they would win, because any Englishman (or Scotsman or Welshman or Irishman) was as good as six—or was it ten?—foreigners. The Sergeant had said so and he'd been out there. It would be a change from these dreary barracks; there was plenty of grog and beautiful native girls—some of them princesses—waiting to throw themselves into your arms. And some fighting. No thought of dirt, disease, discomfort nor, of course, defeat entered their minds. The Army and the nation behind it had plenty of self-confidence.

The Regular Army numbered 213,555 men, of which 26,000 were Irish, and 16,000 Scottish. The Reserve numbered 82,804, the Militia 108,392, the Yeomanry 9,227 and the Volunteers 231,368. This, in theory, meant Britain could put 645,346 men in the field.

This was the army that some fourteen years later made the supreme sacrifice at 'First Ypres'. In the words of Liddell Hart: 'After the battle was over, little survived, save the memory of its spirit.'

General Sir Samuel James Browne, V.C., G.C.B., K.C.S.I.

RECRUITING

In December 1895 Lt.-Col. F. C. Turner, the London District Recruiting Staff Officer, issued the following information.

'There is a contingent of special recruiters. They are paid from two and sixpence to five shillings each for every recruit they bring in, the lower sum being the infantry rate, while the five shillings is paid for Cavalry, Guards and Artillery recruits. They get as much as £2 to £3 for a Life Guardsman. Amongst the Londoners the Cavalry, Highlanders (or Scotch Highlanders as the London recruit calls them) and the Rifle Brigade are in particular demand, the hardest recruits to get being those for Garrison Artillery, for which men of exceptional physique are required, while the branch is not particularly popular. With recruits for the Royal Engineers a special course is taken as they have to be tested in their knowledge of a trade. In the case of a Royal Engineer, too, a certificate of character is required, and the same qualification is necessary in regard to the Army Staff Corps and the Medical Staff Corps. But with the line or cavalry recruit, provided there is nothing of a suspicious nature about him, such as a recruiting officer can generally detect at a glance, a character is not considered a sine qua non.'

Colonel Turner continues regretfully:

'The greatest drawback to recruiting in this country is undoubtedly the British mother. The average British lad has certainly no repugnance to the Army and the average British father has very little objection to his son becoming a soldier. But to the British mother—of the lower middle class more especially—it seems to come as a great blow to find that her boy has not done the great things expected of him and has, as she thinks, sunk to the level of a mere recruit. When I was in charge at St George's barracks I repeatedly had two and three mothers in one day making tearful enquiries after their sons and begging me to help them to get a discharge.'

The recruit could be bought out within the first three months for £10—if anyone happened to have that large sum for those days.

Assessing character at a glance.

TO THOSE ABOUT TO ENLIST

By One Who has Tried It

NO! I am *not* going to offer you *Punch's* famous advice; but at the same time you will find a few 'don'ts' in the course of this attempt at a few useful hints for intending warriors. A not inconsiderable number of young men join the Army under the impression that they are embarking on a glorious life, the principal *motifs* of which are a red coat, bands of music, well-oiled hair, jingling spurs may-be, and a free kit and rations, and any amount of enthusiasm and admiration from a grateful country, and the girls in particular. You get the free kit and rations, such as they are, but you have to earn them, and there is something besides swaggering down the streets of your native town on furlough, before you have got through your recruit drill. So at the outset don't set off with the idea that your soldiering will be all beer and skittles. There is, I believe, a popular notion, fostered by song-writers and eminent novelists, that the soldier is 'gay and free and full of glee,' and all the rest of it, but allow something for poetic licence and 'colour,' and you will be wise. The recruiting sergeant talks smoothly, insinuatingly, nay, respectfully, to you, perchance he will take refreshment at your expense, but—he is a very different individual when you meet him on the parade ground. The man with a stripe on his arm is your superior officer, until you attain his rank, and you had best not forget this interesting fact. Discipline, *toujours* discipline, is the motto and the backbone of the Service, and the recruit very soon discovers so, but it is better for him if he is aware of it at the outset. And here, I may remark, Volunteers often, at the outset of their 'regular' career, take to soldiering with a very bad grace. They have seen just enough of the life to fancy it, and to fancy it is what it is not—a kind of pastime and holiday. They have never been thoroughly in hand or under proper military discipline, and they imagine they can jaw a Regular non-com. as they may have done the sergeant of their company when volunteering.

'Beany' young men are soon undeceived, and they are very unhappy until they have learnt to obey the bridle. No doubt it is not very pleasant to be at the beck and call of every man who wears a stripe on his arm. It may be you have until lately occupied a far more important position in the scale of social life than this man ever has; you may be a better man yourself in the matter of birth, education, physique, and everything else; but he is your superior, and there the whole gist of the thing lies. The youngster who is civil, obliging, and properly deferential (he need not be servile) to the orders of his officer, sergeant, corporal, or senior soldier will get on. The recruit who grows too big for his boots will find they pinch and pinch hard.

Many a lad who has seen twelve months' active service as a Volunteer joins the Army, and comes down to the regiment or depôt thinking he knows everything. He does not require to be taught anything, thank you. And he is quickly taught a vast deal, and taught it in a rather harsh manner, too. Know nothing when you first get into the barrack-room, or on the drill ground, or in the riding school. You will find men who are paid to teach you, and you can follow their instructions and learn as quickly as you like. Old soldiers are always generous to a youngster who admits his rawness and wishes to be taught, the smart know-all gets left every time. Numerous pleasantries will be played on your inexperience. There are certain stereotyped japes, sacred by long usage, that are bound to be worked off on every Johnny Raw. Don't get vexed; remember the man who is grinning at your discomfiture has been through the mill himself, and that you will be putting a wretched recruit under the same torture some day.

Can you work? Be quite sure whether you can before you enlist. The man who comes into the Service with the idea of putting in an easy existence has the hardest life imaginable. He had much better drift quietly into the workhouse and luxuriate in picking oakum or breaking stones. Fondness, or at any rate capacity, for work is a *sine quâ non* the man who intends to be a soldier must possess. One night, as the men of my troop were all busily engaged in preparing accoutrements and clothing for a big parade next day, two recruits were ushered into the room by the orderly corporal. They were welcomed in the rough but genial manner of soldiers and shown their cots, which were made down for them by an old hand. One fellow sat down, and, lighting his pipe, gazed placidly at us whilst we worked. The other, a smart, well-dressed lad, evidently of the better class, approached an old hand somewhat awkwardly. 'I don't know much about your work,' he said, 'but I can black boots.' And he did so, and went straight to the hearts of the room at once, whilst the other, a hulking fellow who had evidently been picked out of the gutter, was marked as a loafer and no good at the same instant. Therefore, if you are lucky enough to have got through your own work, never grudge a helping hand to a comrade.

Elbow grease is the greatest gift a soldier can possess. It *is* a gift. Some men are always working, 'rifting' or 'grafting' as the Army has it, and yet are not as clean as the man who finishes his work in half the time. Knack is the great thing, and can only be acquired by experience. The old hand 'puts up' his saddle, burnished like a new shilling, before the recruit has sponged all his leather-work; and then the raw one is unhappy, and does one of two things. He either works steadily on, taking advice and picking up hints by eye or ear, until he can do his work properly, or he goes in for scamping the job and sooner or later is found out and has a very bad time, and, worst of all, is a marked man in future. Watch an old soldier, one who has the reputation of a 'clean man,' and take him as your model; and always remember the smart, clean, experienced man can do, and does do, things that are not becoming to a newly-joined rookie. Once you are in thorough trim, it is easy to keep so. Remember this, and bear it in mind in respect to your kit. Get your arms, your belts, your saddlery, and your horse—if you are a cavalry man—thoroughly clean, and you will be astonished at the ease with which you can keep them so. Don't burnish over rust—it won't bear looking at—but once get the metal-work *thoroughly* clean and a rub of oil, a suspicion of bath brick, and your bit shines like a new dollar. A reputation for 'tickiness' (dirtiness)—the very worst, indeed, it is possible for a soldier to obtain—is easily earned and never got rid of.

You will not be overpowered at the extent of your wealth as a private soldier. Month in, month out, you will be lucky to draw five shillings a week after deductions for mess allowances, barrack damages, renovation of kit, etc. How you will invest all this great sum is a matter on which I shall not presume to offer you any advice. You can easily get rid of it at the canteen, and will find a considerable number of jolly fellows to assist at that operation. You can expend it in improving your *menu*, or can put it in the regimental savings bank. You can gamble it away, or perchance increase it at cards—I do not recommend either—or send it home to your friends. Personally I found I required all my pay, and a little more, to keep me in grub. A beneficent nation allows you three-quarters of a pound of meat and one pound of bread per diem, and anything else you require, you must pay for yourself. The meat varies as to quality—occasionally it is excellent, less often it is not fit for human consumption. As a rule the bread is fairly good. Groceries and vegetables come out of the mess fund, to which you pay a certain sum from your pay, whether you wish it or not. To sum up, if you are addicted to the pleasures of the table, you must be prepared to mortify your predilection. With careful husbanding, however, you can make your pay sufficient for a few inexpensive luxuries—necessities you would call them in civil life—an occasional quart of beer now and again, and for replenishing your kit. Remember when your small kit—brushes, underclothing, boots, etc.—are worn out or lost, you have to replace them with Government articles at your own cost, and such replacements are deducted from your pay. Government finds you in uniform and boots at stated intervals; meantime, if you lose or destroy such, you have to make them good at your own expense.

You will require some relaxation. How will you take it? You can put on your walking-out uniform, get a pass till 12.0 midnight, and go on the spree with a few particular chums. This may end up in a row with civilians, the police or provost, and mean drill, cells or prison, or, on the other hand, it may be only a swelled head next morning. You can go out and have a rational quiet evening with a comrade or civilian friends, if you prefer to, of course. You can spend the evening at the regimental recreation room or at the canteen. At the latter place, always well managed and worked on co-operative principles, you have cheap and good drink, and where is the corps without vocal talent? As a general rule it is much better, safer, and more economical to pass your evening at your own fireside—the regimental canteen—than to loaf round the low-class public-houses of your town. And here a word as to publicans' behaviour to the uniform. Some, I know, object to soldiers entering their houses; but, as a rule, 'if' the soldier respects his uniform, civilians and publicans also do likewise. You will often hear soldiers of a certain class boasting how they went out without a cent and came back 'skinning drunk.' This feat is easily performed. Many civilians are very generous to the uniform in that respect, but I venture to hope you are not likely to prove a soldier of this kind, in other words, a drunken sponger. You can take a drink from a civilian without losing your self-respect, and the civilian should be aware that as a rule Tommy Atkins cannot always reciprocate.

Don't be in too big a hurry for promotion. If you merit it, you are bound to gain it in the Army, sooner, perhaps, than in any other walk of life; and remember that when it comes it will not be a bed of roses. Every step higher incurs certain responsibilities, and the first step of all is the most important.

A lance-corporal is the hardest worked, most abused, and unhappiest man alive.

Remember when you get that stripe sewn on your sleeve, that yesterday you were plain Private Tommy, and don't fancy yourself Adjutant-General all in a moment. You will have a roughish time at first, especially with the men who were your equals yesterday, and now is the time to show what you are made of. You will require courage, tact, firmness—in a word, a strong heart—if you are to be a success as Lance Jack. The men watch you, and those above watch you, and you had better watch yourself closest of all.

If you can go through a corporal's probation successfully, you will do. After this trial, your course should be fairly smooth, and you can certainly look forward to promotion as vacancies occur and seniority entitles you. There are plenty of good billets in the Service for the right men, and if you do not remain long enough to reach the highest rank attainable to the man who enlists as private—I allude to the higher non-commissioned posts—you will at any rate leave the Service a far more useful member of society than when you entered.

I have barely touched the skirts of my subject, but my few hints may be of service to those whom they are primarily intended for. Implicit obedience, determination to work, sobriety and good humour, are the points indicated, and the qualities absolutely essential for a youngster intending to do well in the Army. Let him go in with his eyes open, and determine to exercise these qualities, which are also absolutely necessary for success in civilian life, and at the expiration of his service—be it short or long—like the writer, he will not regret the time spent as a private soldier.

They have just joined—the soldiers of tomorrow.

THROUGH THE MILITIA

By a

Military Tutor

Woolwich and Sandhurst are not the only channels by which young men can work their way up to commissions in the Army. The hardy and determined aspirant may enlist as a private soldier, and if he has tact, temper, a good digestion, and a slice of luck, he may rise to a commission through the non-commissioned grades. The Militia is another, and a much more pleasant avenue by which the same end may be attained, and it is on and about that well-frequented road that I offer the following remarks:

The Militia, as a channel into the regular service, has been described as a 'back door' and a 'side wind'. Confusion of metaphor aptly illustrates the mental state of persons uttering these libels, which I make bold to say, are as groundless as they are ridiculous. How then came it to pass that these expressions have been frequently heard in conversation and read in print? I will tell you. They originated with the old civilian tutors and schoolmasters who, utterly dense and ignorant on military matters, and fearing that their craft was in danger, decried any ordeal for army candidates other than their own book work. These interesting fossils were encouraged by a few petrified officers who, having passed by what they called 'the right way', had no toleration for anything not branded R.M.A. or R.M.C. But the days of that Egyptian darkness are happily ended, the Militiamen who enter the first line having proved themselves no whit behind their brother officers of the same standing.

The *quondam* cadet is, in all probability, better posted up in literary subjects, but the militiaman has the advantage in age, practical knowledge of men and matters military, and generally in sportsmanlike qualifications. Comparatively few of either class rise to be generals; it should therefore be our object to obtain a flow of strong, sound, sensible and fairly educated young gentlemen, capable of earning the respect of the men, and of performing creditably the duties of regimental officers. Neither is it desirable that they should be all of one pattern, a consummation which is wisely obviated by alternative methods of admission.

When a fond parent has been irresistibly led to the conclusion that the boy whom he destines for a soldier's career has more aptitude for practical work than for abstract study, he will probably determine to send him through the Militia. This involves two annual trainings as a subaltern in the latter force, and a period spent at a military tutor's, sufficiently long to ensure his passing an examination in military law, tactics, fortification, and topography. The militia regiment and the crammer are important items which often decide the bent and bias of young Hopeful's future life, and parents cannot be too careful, or take too great pains, to secure an unimpeachable regiment and a conscientious crammer. When a youth sees himself for the first time in war paint, and is introduced to a mess and other novelties of regimental life, it is of the utmost moment that he should not be deceived by erroneous precept, or misled by unsafe example; that he should not mistake coarseness for wit, or regard rowdyism as the legitimate outcome of a cheerful temperament.

Eschew a regiment in which the practical joker flourishes; he is a sure sign that the colonel and adjutant are not up to their business. A good commanding officer soon weeds out those objectionable men who bring discredit on their cloth; he has an eye to the moral and social as well as to the military fitness of his officers, his battalion is in a good state of discipline, and his will, which is at once kindly and firm, makes itself felt by all ranks, from the senior major to the junior drummer. It is a privilege and a valuable preparatory lesson for an Army candidate to serve, even for a short time, under that kind of commanding officer, and there are many such in the old constitutional force. But there are other sorts as well; for instance, the easy-going variety who places himself unreservedly in the hands of his adjutant, a course of conduct which infallibly spoils the adjutant and keeps the senior officers in a state of chronic disgust. That colonel's battalion is uncomfortable, and should be avoided. Then there is the convivially genial C.O. who makes things rather too comfortable for the time being, but whose regiment is a bad school for a young man having his own way to make in the Army.

The much-married C.O. must not be forgotten. He is himself under the command of a wife whose firm conviction is that the band, the officers, especially the juniors, and, in fact, the whole show, exist for no other purpose than the supply of amusement to herself and her friends. Her husband and his officers must obey her behests as to dances, picnics, water parties, land parties, and different kinds of displays, all of which, including the annual inspection, she patronises as if a supreme position belonged to her without the remotest possibility of question. Sometimes it is with the greatest difficulty she is prevented from issuing her orders on parade. When this is tried on, the lady has to be effectively thwarted, with all available tact of course, but she likes it not, and avenges herself afterwards by giving the colonel a bad quarter of an hour. The incidental expenses in a battalion so commanded are, for the majority of candidates, prohibitory.

In a good and smart regiment of Militia the tone prevailing among the officers is a mellow blend, suggestive at once of the soldier and the country gentleman. County families of the first rank are represented in it, and county houses are open to the last-joined subaltern, whether he hails from London or a Colony, whether he is a son of a rich neighbour or of an unknown Vicar in a remote corner of the land. It is always understood that the Colonel's acceptance of an officer for his regiment, is a guarantee that he is presentable, and it is quite certain that the early training and experiences of Militia subalterns, while out with their regiments, have been of the greatest service to them from a social point of view, and have often had an effect on the formation of character and manner, not elsewhere obtainable. I am speaking of good battalions and good counties. In such a battalion the duty is carried on with precision and in strict accordance with the regulations, and as an immense amount of work is got through in the four weeks of training, not to speak of the period of preliminary drill, the newly-joined subaltern gets a more thorough insight into the details of soldiering, and learns more about his profession than he will ever again do in any four weeks of his service.

The trainings furnish him with practical illustrations of, and throw new light upon, the four subjects studied at his tutor's, especially on law and tactics. He becomes intelligent on the matters of pay, clothing, boots, necessaries, marching money, and the thousand details of interior economy that cannot be understood except by personal contact with them. Probably he may be brigaded with a line battalion or with another of Militia, and have an opportunity of learning the unwritten as well as the written laws which govern the intercourse of officers and troops. As a matter of course he will lose the stoop of the student, if he had it, and become a well set-up soldier, but his Militia experiences may be expected to have another and permanently healthy influence on his future life, in that they will strengthen his interest in field sports and manly exercise. There are but few regiments in the constitutional force that do not number among the gentlemen who sit around the mess table, well-known performers on the moor, in the hunting field, or on the river either as oars or anglers. Altogether the education received by a candidate when passing through this channel, is generally fitted to produce a very desirable officer, and such is the view taken by the majority of Army Colonels.

I now propose that inquiring parents should resign themselves to my care, to be personally conducted through some of the highways and byways of cramming. The ordinary crammer who prepares boys for their literary examinations does not come within my scope. I treat solely of the great instructional corps of retired officers, ranging in rank from general to lieutenant, who impart the results of their own study and experience to Militia candidates for the Army. The needful knowledge of the four military subjects already mentioned is, speaking generally, possessed by all officers, but it exists sometimes in an ill-arranged form, and the power of conveying it to others is wanting. It requires not merely a well-instructed officer, but a man of ability and a good organizer to make an Army tutor, and even then some accidental circumstance may cause his failure. Successful men in this line must therefore be credited with considerable grit; they are entitled to our respect, and, considering the material on which they have to work, to our sympathy also. The mammoth crammers whose advertisements fill whole pages, week after week, in the service journals, have the ball at their foot. They are so widely known that nothing but the grossest mismanagement or the most cruel bad luck can drag them down from their pre-eminence; but the officer who is comparatively unknown, and whose connection is small, has an uphill fight. Unless possessed of capital, his better plan, and one which he frequently adopts, is to engage himself as an instructor in one of the larger establishments. In that way he has no financial responsibility, he gains experience, and probably sees his way, after a year or two, to start on his own account. Private places of instruction for the Army are somewhat analogous to private ship-building yards doing naval work. Both of them turn out good workmanship, and greatly increase the warlike power of the country.

The great tutorial establishments have this advantage, that they admit of their students being classified according to their proficiency. An expert can also be entrusted with the tuition in each subject. On the other hand the proprietor of a very small establishment, who does all the work without assistance, may be trusted to give the utmost individual attention to his pupils, and to leave no stone unturned to ensure their passing. But after all, it is on the perseverance and mental stamina of the candidate himself that his success or failure chiefly depends. The regulated text books may be read and lucidly expounded; the questions set in past examinations may be inquisitively scanned; test examinations may be undergone and wrong answers corrected, but unless the student has learned to master his intellectual powers and to concentrate them on the subject in hand, it is little better than a toss-up whether he will get through or not.

If the Army tutor is married and allows pupils to live in his house, it will generally be found advantageous for the pupil to be his 'paying guest'. It will most certainly be so if the tutor, in addition to being a good disciplinarian, is a man of high character and principle. It is almost too much for any one man, however, both to instruct and to take the out-of-study supervision. The latter is usually considered the more trying duty of the two, as the young gentlemen occupy a kind of debatable ground between boyhood and manhood, which makes it most difficult to maintain the golden mean between a tight hand and a loose rein, and some of them combine all the coltish tricks of a youngster with more than the assurance of an old man. Sometimes their vagaries take a foolish but seldom a vicious form. One of the foolish order may, for example, affect an ultra sporting kit which he wears with a knowing, horsy air, but the practised eye can detect a tinge of green in the turnout, and the wearer looks as if he were unmistakably safer on his feet than on a horse. Another foolish specimen whose family has within recent years made money in trade, and small blame to them, informs his auditors, in season and out of season, that he is a gentleman. He does not usually look like one, and he is perhaps afraid that if he does not advertise the fact it will be forgotten. There are times, too, when less amusing and more offensive traits are exhibited, as, for instance, when an incorrigibly self-assertive youth makes a point of picking up and combating every remark made by his tutor or instructors, not in the spirit of Mr. Midshipman Easy, but apparently in one of animosity and contradiction. That individual may be bracketed with the smasher of furniture and promoter of rows; the one is as great a nuisance as the other, and after due warning, should be promptly drafted.

I remember the case of a Militia subaltern who closed his term of residence at his tutor's, in what was at the time, considered a very cool and calm sort of way. On the day before his departure he took French leave and stayed out all night. Returning in the morning before his tutor was awake, he left on the drawing-room table two cards inscribed (say) 'Mr. John Jones, 3rd Battalion Blankshire Regiment, P.P.C.,' and went off in a cab with his portmanteau. The facilities existing in the metropolis for undetected evil-doing increase the cares of the London Crammer who looks after the conduct of his pupils. If the candidate does not live in the tutor's house, he ought certainly to have some 'guide, philosopher and friend' who will keep him from forgetting the duties of a Christian gentleman, for no safeguard should be neglected at the opening of life, when impressions are so readily formed, and every aid should be offered towards the formation of a true and strong character.

Although 'the child is father to the man', it would be unfair to judge the man from the actions of the boy. A good regiment and a few added years of life make most young officers into men in all senses of the word. They have outgrown the peculiar ailments of their hobbledehoyhood, just as they did those of their infancy; they look back with a laugh at the sporting rig with which they astonished the denizens of their neighbourhood, with a sigh of regret at their unmannerly and contradictory antics, and with a blush of shame at their more serious escapades. I have seldom been more gratified than I was when in the company of an Army tutor a short time ago. A gentleman came up and in my presence named the tutor and announced his own name. After a few cordial words on both sides, the younger man said: 'I have just come home from India on leave. I have often felt sorry for the trouble I gave you in the old days, and I determined to tell you so the first time I saw you.' That had been a contradictory and argumentative boy, but I think my readers will agree that he had now become a man. And I am sure that many officers now serving in all parts of the world have a kind and grateful remembrance of their Army tutor, and are proud of the fact that they have passed into the Army 'through the Militia'.

PERSONALITIES

Opposite

H.R.H. The Duke of Cambridge, K.G., K.T., K.P., G.C.B., G.C.S.I., G.C.M.G.

The Duke of Cambridge was born in 1819, and entered the Army in 1837, with the rank of Colonel. He became Major-General in 1845, Lieut.-General in 1854, General in 1856, Field Marshal in 1862. In the Crimea the Duke commanded the 1st division and was present at the Alma, Balaclava and at Inkerman, where he had his horse shot under him. In July, 1856, the Duke was appointed Commander-in-Chief, which office he held until October last. On his retirement the Duke of Cambridge was specially appointed Chief Personal A.D.C. to the Queen, and Colonel-in-Chief of the Army, a distinction that will give the Duke precedence and an ex-officio position at all reviews and military ceremonies he may be present at.

Commander-in-Chief of the Army for thirty-nine years. This shows an element of continuity which the present-day army lacks.

Opposite

Major-General Lord Methuen, C.B., C.M.G.
This well-known officer entered the Scots Guards in 1864, and has since seen much varied service: in Ashanti in 1873–4; in the Tel-el-Kebir campaign of 1882; and in Bechuanaland, where he commanded 'Methuen's Horse' in 1885. He has also held important staff appointments at the Horse Guards, was for three years Military Attaché in Berlin, and now commands the Home District, where he has done yeoman service on behalf of the Volunteers. Our portrait was taken at Windsor at the recent inspection of the Scots Guards' detachment for Ashanti, before the Queen.

But he was not so happy later in South Africa.

Above

Field-Marshal Wolseley
In 1895 Wolseley became Commander-in-Chief. He was extremely efficient and forward-looking but was not invariably popular. His presence in many campaigns had earned him the nickname 'our only General'. The expression 'All Sir Garnet', long in use, denoted that all arrangements (for anything) were excellent. The solar topee, used up till the beginning of World War II, was known officially as the 'Wolseley helmet'.

Above
Field-Marshal Lord Roberts, V.C., G.C.B.
There is no more popular officer in the Military Service than 'Bobs'. Frederick Sleigh Roberts, the distinguished son of a distinguished father, is an old officer of the Bengal Artillery. In the Mutiny before Delhi, where he was wounded and had his horse shot under him, he repeatedly distinguished himself, and won the V.C. The Umbeylah and Abyssinian Campaigns brought him more credit, and the Afghan War capped it. His march to Candahar assured his position in the front rank. India never has had a more able or successful Commander-in-Chief. Now he is a Peer of the Realm and a Field-Marshal, further progress towards efficiency of the Forces in Ireland is assured in his capable hands.

Field-Marshal Roberts was not only popular but he was also flexible and extremely able. As Commander-in-Chief in South Africa in 1900 he had appalling problems but solved most of them. He received an earldom for his services in South Africa.

Opposite
Lieutenant-General Sir H. Evelyn Wood, V.C., G.C.B., G.C.M.G.
Sir Evelyn Wood began life in the Navy, and served with the Naval Brigade in the Crimea. From Midshipman he became Cornet of Light Dragoons, and then a Lieutenant in the 17th Lancers, while holding which rank he served in the Indian Mutiny and won his V.C. He then exchanged as Captain into the Infantry. The Ashanti War of 1873–4 brought Colonel Wood prominently forward, and he added to his reputation in the Kaffir War of 1878, in Zululand, and in the Egyptian and Khartoum Expeditions, taking part in the latter as Chief of the Staff to Lord Wolseley. After commanding the Eastern District at Home, and at Aldershot, he became Quartermaster-General at Headquarters two years ago.

Sir Evelyn Wood, later a Field-Marshal, so enjoyed the land fighting in the Crimea (in which he was nearly killed) that he transferred to the Army. His record of changing services once and regiments three times, as well as winning a V.C., is unlikely to be surpassed.

21

General Sir Redvers Buller, V.C., G.C.B.

Buller was outstandingly brave, but in the South African campaign
fell short of requirements as an army commander. A kindly man he
deplored actions which might cause casualties among his troops.

Opposite
**General Sir Julius Augustus Robert Raines, K.C.B., Colonel of
'The Buffs'.**
This distinguished officer obtained his first commission in the 3rd
Buffs, at the early age of sixteen, on 28 January 1842, but was
transferred to the 95th Derbyshire Regiment in order to serve with
his father, the late Colonel J. R. Raines, Chevalier of the Order of
St. Louis—a veteran officer who, as an ensign in the 82nd, fought
at Rolica, Vimero and Coruna. The following is a brief summary
of Sir Julius Raines's services: Crimea—Battles of Alma (where, as
a captain, he carried the Queen's colour of the 95th), Inkerman,
and Tchernaya, siege of Sebastopol (wounded), assault on Redan,
June 18. Mentioned in despatches, medal with three clasps,
Sardinian and Turkish medals, 5th class Medjidie, brevet majority.
Indian Mutiny—In command at assault and capture of Rowa, siege
and capture of Awah, commanded 3rd assaulting column at
capture of Kotah, battle of Gwalior, capture of city and fortress
of Gwalior (wounded), capture of Powree, and action of Kundrye.
Five times mentioned in despatches, medal with clasp, promoted
lieutenant-colonel, brevet of colonel, and C.B. Expedition into
Arabia, 1865–6—Commanded the expedition from Aden, capture
of several towns and forts. Received the commendation of the
Commander-in-Chief at Bombay 'for the efficient manner in which
these successful operations were carried out'. Sir Julius has
commanded the 95th Regiment for thirteen years.

'The Buffs' were the East Kent Regiment and are now the 4th
battalion of the Queen's Regiment. Even at the age of 71 the
General appears to have lost none of his grip.

Above

General Lord Chelmsford, G.C.B.

Entering the army in 1844, Lord Chelmsford was first under fire in the Crimea, where, as a captain in the Grenadier Guards, he served in the trenches before Sebastopol. With the 95th foot, as Lieutenant-Colonel, he served in India during the Mutiny; a few years after that he again saw service in the field as Deputy Adjutant General of the expeditionary force in Abyssinia—winning the C.B. appointment as A.D.C. to the Queen, and mention in despatches for 'great ability and untiring energy'. From 1868 to 1876 he filled the high position of Adjutant General in India, and after that, after commanding brigades at Shorncliffe and Aldershot, in 1878 he went to the Cape as Commander-in-Chief. There he first brought the Kaffir War to a satisfactory end, being promoted to K.C.B. for his services, and then took charge of the operations of the Zulu War, conducting that memorable campaign to its successful close at Ulundi, where Lord Chelmsford was in personal command on the battlefield. The Zulu War made Lord Chelmsford a G.C.B., and he was finally promoted to full General in 1888.

Opposite

The Constable of the Tower.

It is as long ago as sixty-three years since Sir Daniel Lysons, then eighteen, entered the Army as an ensign in the First Royals. He saw his first service in Canada in the 'thirties', at the time of the rebellion, a period of which, in his recently published reminiscences, Sir Daniel has many stirring tales to tell. Between that and war service before the enemy in the Crimea, came a long spell of duty in America and the West Indies. In 1861, Sir Daniel was again in Canada, charged with organizing the Canadian Militia in connection with the Trent affair. Sir Daniel Lysons in 1880 was appointed to the Aldershot Command, and six years ago he was made Constable of the Tower. In his day 'Dodgy Dan', as he used to be called, was considered second to none as a tactician. He is Colonel of the 'Sherwood Foresters'.

Hudson & Kearns.
London, S.E.

The Provost Marshal at Aldershot. His eyes have a look of permanent disbelief that must have developed from hearing hundreds of improbable excuses.

Mr. G. D. A. Fleetwood Wilson, C.B.
Assistant Under-Secretary of State for War, entered the Civil Service in 1870; became Director of Army Clothing in 1893, and Assistant Under-Secretary of State in 1898. Created C.B. in 1891. Is a J.P. for the County of London.

Opposite
General Sir John Alexander Ewart, K.C.B.
Few officers now alive have acquitted themselves with such distinction as the subject of this sketch, now Colonel of the Argyll and Sutherland Highlanders. Sir John served with the 93rd Highlanders in the Crimea, and was present at the Alma, Balaklava, and the siege of Sebastopol, receiving the Crimean medal with four clasps, the Sardinian and Turkish medals, the 5th class Medjidie, and Inkerman, being made a Knight of the Legion of Honour. During the Indian Mutiny he gave evidence of exceptional bravery when leading the first party of stormers at Secunderbagh. On this occasion he captured one of the enemy's colours, receiving at the same time two sabre wounds. At Cawnpore his left arm was carried away by a cannon shot, and he narrowly escaped with his life. He was mentioned in despatches of 16 January 1858, was thanked for his services by the Governor General in Council, was made a C.B. and A.D.C. to the Queen. Sir John was Lieutenant-Colonel of the 78th Highlanders for over five years. He was made a K.C.B. in June, 1887.

He was one of 'the thin red line' which saved the port of Balaclava in the Crimean War.

Hudson & Kearns

TRAINING AND BARRACKS LIFE

In the Army men spend much of their time developing skills they may never use. Army training is designed to produce maximum casualties to the enemy at minimum cost to oneself. However, any casualties which occur in training are a disaster and, even when injuries are slight, lead to tedious courts of enquiry or even court martials. Nevertheless instant obedience, reflexive instincts and meticulous thoroughness have to be instilled. There can be no half-measures in the Army; either you shoot straight and kill or you are probably killed yourself; you conceal yourself properly or fail to do so with dire consequences.

To the soldier much of his training appears time-wasting idiocy. He digs a trench in the morning, and fills it in the afternoon. In the nineteenth century it was rare for anyone to explain any exercise or form of training to soldiers; the 'need to communicate' concept has only developed since World War II. Inevitably there are long periods in which the soldier is merely waiting. Some cynics believe that officers wait till rain is forecast, then arrange exercises.

On active service, as on the North West frontier or in the Soudan, it was an entirely different matter. The first bullet whistling by a man's ears—if he was lucky and it did not go between them—resulted in an entirely different attitude, though after a time men could grow careless and need further training.

The climax of peacetime training was manoeuvres, in which armies were pitted against armies with umpires to record the score. Reputations could be made or lost on manoeuvres, and for senior officers this could be a vital factor in promotion prospects.

Photographers in the nineteenth century were able to wander freely, but, being short of transport for their equipment, usually concentrated their efforts in rear areas. Military correspondents, however, tended to be where the bullets were thickest. As photographic equipment became more portable, photographers began to take almost incredible pictures; inevitably they suffered casualties in doing so.

Here the clearest pictures are carefully posed; pictures taken on manoeuvres tend to be dark and blurred.

Sapper balloonists

Wagons carrying balloons and gas

Crowning the balloon

Balloon partly full

Taking an observation

A balloon section of the Royal Engineers was established in 1890.
In 1894 it found a permanent home in South Farnborough,
Hampshire. Four balloon sections saw action against the Boers,
achieving their best results when directing the fire of British
artillery at Magersfontein and Lombard's Kop. The gas for the
balloons was made by applying sulphuric acid to granulated zinc.

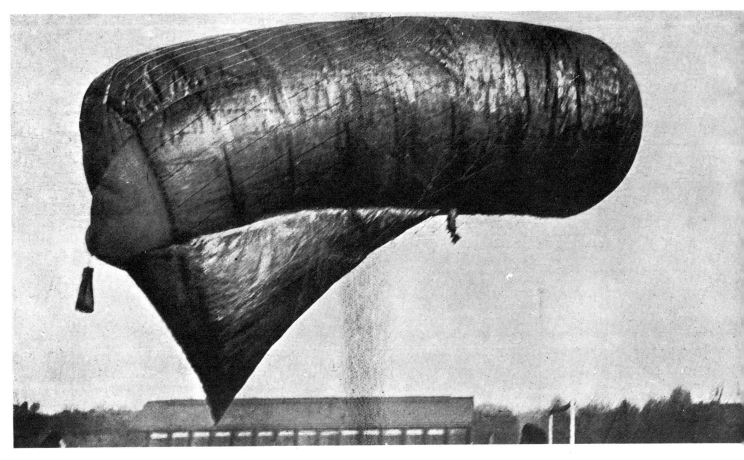

Giving the balloon a trial trip

The new military balloon at Aldershot

The trouble with balloons is that they look so slovenly and
unsoldierly.

Military cyclists. Bicycle drill. Later these bicycles would be closely
aligned wheel to wheel, almost spoke to spoke.

The South Lancashire's cyclists preparing for a ride

The South Lancashires had a distinguished military record — though
not on bicycles.

Firing an 110-ton gun with powder

Sections of shell made in the Royal Laboratory

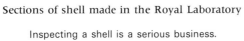

Inspecting a shell is a serious business.

A gun afloat

The Royal Horse Artillery transporting guns across the Liffey on improvised rafts.

Maxim Guns in Action
In almost every recent campaign, whether great or small, machine-guns have played an important part. They have been conspicuous both on account of their extreme mobility and alarming destructive power. As an adjunct to infantry they are invaluable, and one or two may now be found attached to almost every battalion. That their worth is fully appreciated by the Authorities may be gathered from the fact that at the recent Royal Review at Aldershot, battalions armed with these deadly weapons appeared with them on parade. Unlike artillery, however (with which machine-guns must not be confused), the Maxim, now king of machine-guns, can be drawn a considerable distance by the machine-gun detachment without the assistance of a mule or horse. On any field day it may be seen careering over hill and dale at 'the double', drawn by draft animals of the human species, coming into action belching forth a shower of lead, and then moving on to another position of vantage. Such work is trying at home, but it is even more so in Malta and other tropical climates, where the British soldier at his best is not too energetic.

Hasty entrenchments

Topographical classes

Some further elements of Sandhurst life are presented here. At the top is a working party of cadets engaged, under the superintendence of an instructor, in digging rifle pits and shelter trenches. They are artistically akin to Mr. Ruskin's batch of undergraduates who did navvy work at Hinksey, near Oxford, a number of years ago. The motive idea was that to make a road was quite as aesthetic as to pull an oar, and much more productive. However that may be, there is no doubt that pick and shovel work brings out solid qualities, and teaches officers duly to estimate the efforts of Tommy Atkins in like circumstances. The next picture is composed of two topographical classes equipped for a surveying excursion; and the last shows cadets practising on the rifle range, and thus preparing themselves for the intelligent supervision of men who, if they cannot shoot straight, are worse than useless. When it is added that gymnastics and physical drill are not neglected at Sandhurst, it will be seen that a sensible and robust all-round military training is there provided for the future officers of the British cavalry and infantry.

Rifle Range

No. 11 (Field) Company R.E., at bridging practice at the Curragh
The Royal Engineers are organized in two battalions (each of two troops) for bridging and telegraphic work, a Field Depot comprising two 'parks', and in upwards of fifty separate companies specially established as Field Companies, Fortress Companies, Survey, Railway, and Submarine-mining Companies, besides a Coast Battalion of eleven sections and eight Depot Companies. The men we see here at work belong to the 11th (Field) Company now stationed at the Curragh. They are shown throwing a light military bridge across the Liffey. Four of these Field Companies would be told off to an Army Corps, and each is at all times provided with tools, explosives, and technical equipment to undertake operations, such as the construction of field defences, the attack of field fortifications, making or destroying roads, telegraphs, bridges, or railways, and the crossing of small rivers for which special purpose a small section of bridging equipment is carried. Each Field Company comprises one major, one captain, four subalterns, with sergeants, corporals, artificers, sappers, drivers, and wagonmen. It numbers two hundred and thirteen of all ranks, with pontoon and trestle wagons and forge, forage, and tool carts.

This is a perfectly serious picture, although it looks like a stage skit or a 'Punch' joke. In the original caption the duties of the sentry are listed: 'They are not on any account to sing, smoke, or suffer any noise to be made near them, and they are also to keep a watchful eye over all property committed to their charge.' There seems little possibility of this sentry wishing to break the rule about singing.

Stable duty—as posed for the camera.

Behind the shelter trenches

Independent field-firing

These two pictures show the Oxford and Cambridge Volunteer corps
on manoeuvres at Aldershot in 1899. It was bitterly cold and there
were heavy snow-storms. Cambridge were thought to be slightly
the better of the two, certainly the keener.

THE TYPICAL SOLDIER OF TODAY

By Callum Beg

Innumerable changes have of late years taken place in the Army, most of which have proved of benefit to the private soldier. 'Tommy Atkins' of today is better clothed, fed, and in every respect better treated than was his predecessor of twenty or thirty years ago, and it is these very changes which have had the effect of inducing a better class of men to join the profession of arms and at the same time of improving the status of the rank and file.

Those who are out of touch with the Army and all things military are denied the opportunity of observing to what a great extent such seemingly trivial matters permeate the life and manners of soldiers as a class, and are, perhaps, too ready to believe that while in every particular the world continues to progress, Tommy—the one exception proving the rule—remains untouched by the waves of education and philanthropy surging round him on every side.

That we should look on the military with an unfavourable eye is hardly to be expected in a nation such as ours, owing as it does its present opulence and power in every part of the world to an Army at all times second to none.

The cynic may sneer, the moralist may shake the head; but neither can deny that our mighty Empire, upon which the sun never sets, is indebted for much of its mammoth growth to successive centuries of British pluck. Still, by thousands of those whose ancestors have contributed to the building up of this colossal structure over which the Union Jack continues to wave supreme, our soldiers are regarded as a body of dissolute libertines or, at best, as idle and superfluous members of society.

In the days of the Iron Duke it may have been so, nor was dissipation at that date peculiar to military men. Drunkenness and gambling were the vices of the time, common alike to all, but times have changed. We have become more civilized, more refined.

The 'three-bottle' man is a being of the past. He has died a natural death with the stage coach, the pack-horse, and the full-bottomed wig. No longer do our squires spend the night in drunken slumber under the tables at which they quaffed their wine. All these things have changed, and yet many of us are content to believe that the Army remains as it was a hundred years ago.

Comparatively speaking, there is now little drunkenness among soldiers, but the prevalent idea that Tommy is prone to exceed in this respect may be easily explained.

Should he be even slightly inebriated Her Majesty's uniform, from its attractiveness, singles him out from among a crowd of civilians. The tattered coat and moleskin trousers of the loafer may pass unnoticed as he rolls home from the gin palace. Once safely within the threshold he conducts himself according to his own sweet will. He may beat his wife, ill-treat his children, or commit any folly which his besotted brain may conceive, but unless they inform the police, or alarm the neighbours, no greater punishment than a headache awaits him on the following day. Not so with our military friend. Let him show any signs of hilarity on his return to barracks, and the guard-room immediately becomes his temporary home. Here he is obliged to pass the night, nor does his punishment end with this. The following morning he is 'for it',* and, in addition to the authorised fine, may receive other punishment—confinement to barracks, or imprisonment—according to the gravity of the case.

The certainty with which the crime of drunkenness will most surely be visited, causes the soldier to be careful in the extreme. If sufficiently capable to reach his cot in safety he usually retires thereto in preference to reposing in charge of the regimental guard.

It is surely equally erroneous to attribute bad manners to soldiers as a class. With the exception of those who 'go down to the sea in ships' there is no section of the community more polite and courteous, especially towards the weaker sex. If not naturally so, their training is such that from being of necessity respectful to their military superiors, whether officers or non-commissioned officers, they consequently learn to address all with whom they come in contact in a civil and becoming manner.

This is not the opinion of some who cater for the amusement of the populace, in garrison towns, but while these gentlemen continue to treat our soldiers as reptiles it is no matter for surprise that Tommy (in such cases a customer not a *servant*), resents it—at times in a more forceable way than prudence would seem to dictate. The wholesale boycotting of soldiers by those individuals (whose *modus operandi* is so well described in the well-known lines by Rudyard Kipling), is but a short-sighted and illogical policy, but Tommy is not without his champions in all sections of the community, and we trust that the way in which this subject has lately been ventilated in the public press, may be productive of a radical change.

Should one man who has the honour of wearing the Queen's uniform so far forget himself as to disgrace it, there appears nothing in this lamentable incident to establish a bias in favour of another conducting himself in an equally discreditable manner. It is impossible to conceive anything more unjust than the judging of a class by the behaviour of one or two of the members composing it, and in the case of the Army it is especially so, for no profession or trade includes in its ranks individuals drawn from so many different spheres of life.

Some would have us believe that Tommy is ignorant and unfit to associate with those who have adopted other professions. On the contrary, the average soldier can put his civilian brother to shame by evincing a more intimate knowledge of standard literature and history, both political and military; and he may well congratulate himself on being saved the constant companionship of those who, being unlettered themselves, are satisfied to believe, on the authority of their grandparents, that our noble defenders are men of an intellectual calibre inferior to their own. There are in addition to the foregoing a number of arguments against Army Service advanced by young men who, though qualified to enlist, are nevertheless constrained from placing themselves in the hands of the recruiter.

They have been brought up to believe that the Army is badly fed, and no amount of reasoning can convince them that their ideas on this subject are erroneous, but we feel confident that only a very small percentage of those who follow the drum has previous to joining the ranks, regularly enjoyed such substantial and wholesome fare as is daily set before the soldier. Nor is it right to suppose that the Army, as a whole, is overworked.

If we except Aldershot, and one or two other large Military camps, there are but few stations where not only the evening but the greater part of the afternoon is available for such amusement as Tommy may care to select.

*For the Orderly Room.

Numbers of men shun Army Service on the plea that the soldier is treated by his superiors as little better than a dog, and too many are ready to believe it. The severe discipline which formerly existed has, however, given way to a code more in keeping with modern ideas of humanity, and corporal punishment has been entirely abolished. Formerly, for the most trivial offence, a soldier was confined in the guard-room until disposed of by his commanding officer, but that institution is now exclusively reserved for the drunken and insubordinate.

The punishment awarded by commanding officers is, almost without exception, proportionate to the crime, and seldom exceeds ten days' confinement to barracks. In more serious cases a term of '168 hours' imprisonment' is given, and an offender is only remanded for trial by court-martial when the commanding officer is of opinion that the amount of punishment which he is authorised to award is inadequate to meet the wants of the case, or when its nature renders trial indispensable. At home there are three species of courts-martial, viz., regimental, district, and general.

The second is now the most common. It is empowered to award a sentence of two years' imprisonment and 'discharge with ignominy'. Soldiers are only tried by general court-martial when the crime of which they are accused is exceptionally grave. This Court may pass a sentence of death or penal servitude, but the former is practically unknown except on active service.

As regards the treatment of soldiers by company officers and non-commissioned officers, there is little to which the most fastidious could take exception. The officers of the British Army are, doubtless, kinder and more considerate to those under them than their brethren on the Continent, and take an interest in the welfare and amusements of their men which is totally unknown in France or Germany.

It is no uncommon thing to find officers and men playing football and cricket together, or cooperating with each other in giving entertainments, such as concerts and theatricals.

Dances given by the sergeants of a regiment are invariably attended by the colonel and officers, who are generally willing to be present at such gatherings when given by corporals or privates serving under them. In fact a most satisfactory feeling of *bon cameraderie* pervades all ranks of our Army, and it is, indeed, rare to find an officer who is not only respected, but regarded as a brother-in-arms by those whom it is his duty to command. Were the discipline obtaining in the Army at the present day infinitely more severe, it would, by no means, affect a man of exemplary conduct, inasmuch as the rigour of military law is exclusively felt by those who transgress its precepts. Leave to remain out of barracks until midnight is unsparingly granted to all well-behaved men who apply for a pass to their company officer the day before it is required. Under certain conditions a *permanent* pass may be obtained, which entitles the holder to this privilege every night, when not on duty, without making fresh application. In fine, Tommy is treated by his military superiors in a way which leaves little to be desired.

Scanty remuneration is set forth as an additional objection by many eligible men, but we would leave our readers to decide whether there are, in other walks of life, young men of eighteen or twenty years who can, without 'thought for the morrow', dispose of four or five shillings per week on other than the necessities of life.

After all deductions have been made, a well-behaved soldier can rely on receiving this sum, which increases regularly as he grows older in the Service of the Queen.

It is frequently asserted that promotion is within the reach of none but the educated classes of the community, and that the recruit who has missed the advantages of a sound intellectual training must consequently 'go to the wall'.

Undoubtedly, no one is raised to the position of non-commissioned officer until he has evinced sufficient amount of knowledge to entitle him to this envied rank, but, as the Army schools at every station are open to soldiers without the payment of a fee, there is no excuse for one who remains in an inferior position owing to an imperfect acquaintance with the three elementary 'R's', so easily acquired after a few months of diligent application. Perhaps the commonest argument advanced against enlistment is the supposed difficulty to be met with when seeking employment on return to civilian life. It cannot be denied that our streets are full of unemployed men of the Army Reserve, but if enquiry be made it will in all probability transpire that by far the greater part of these is composed of individuals of doubtful character, or of men who have failed to make the best of their opportunities, and it is not, therefore, owing to their having 'served' that throws them for support on the charity of their fellowmen.

In these days when so many lucrative situations under Government are open to ex-soldiers, it should be easy for any well-conducted man to obtain employment after discharge, but accidents are bound to happen even to the most deserving. If it be our misfortune, to encounter at any time a 'Son of the Empire' starving and cold through no fault of his own, we will the more easily solve the problem by attributing his lamentable condition to the irony of Fate rather than by laying the responsibility upon the noble profession to which he had formerly belonged.

Above

A dismounted lancer at a skirmishing display

Here we have a picture which will serve to remind many of our readers of the Military Displays at the Agricultural Hall, and to others will explain the kind of fighting which Dr. Jameson's troopers made with the Boers at Krugerdorp. It is a pretty idea, teaching a cavalry horse to lie down and serve as a living screen, from behind which his rider can fire in safety, and moreover, has its use in warfare. In the present instance the dismounted horseman (Rough-rider Corporal Long, of the 17th Lancers) is one of a line of skirmishers ordered to use their carbines on foot, against an enemy whom they are unable to get at owing to the nature of intervening obstacles.

The horse appears to be thinking 'he won't find it as easy as this in 1899'. After some sharp lessons from the Boers, the role of cavalry became increasingly that of mounted infantry.

Opposite

A veterinary demonstration – 1st Life Guards

The Staff of Farriers in a cavalry regiment belong to the department of which the Regimental Veterinary Surgeon is the head, and the scope of their duties thus includes practically everything that has to do with the care of the horses in sickness, as well as with their efficiency and general fitness for service in regards to shoes and equipment. In the photograph which forms the subject of our illustration, we have Farrier Wallace of 1st Life Guards, showing the skull of a horse, demonstrating the disease from which the animal died, in the presence of an officer of the same regiment, Lieutenant the Marquiss of Hamilton.

The Marquis might well look non-committal. The unfortunate horse, which has lost the rest of its bones as well as its flesh, appears to have had trouble with its nose. It is not clear whether this is an open-air post-mortem or an officers' instructional period.

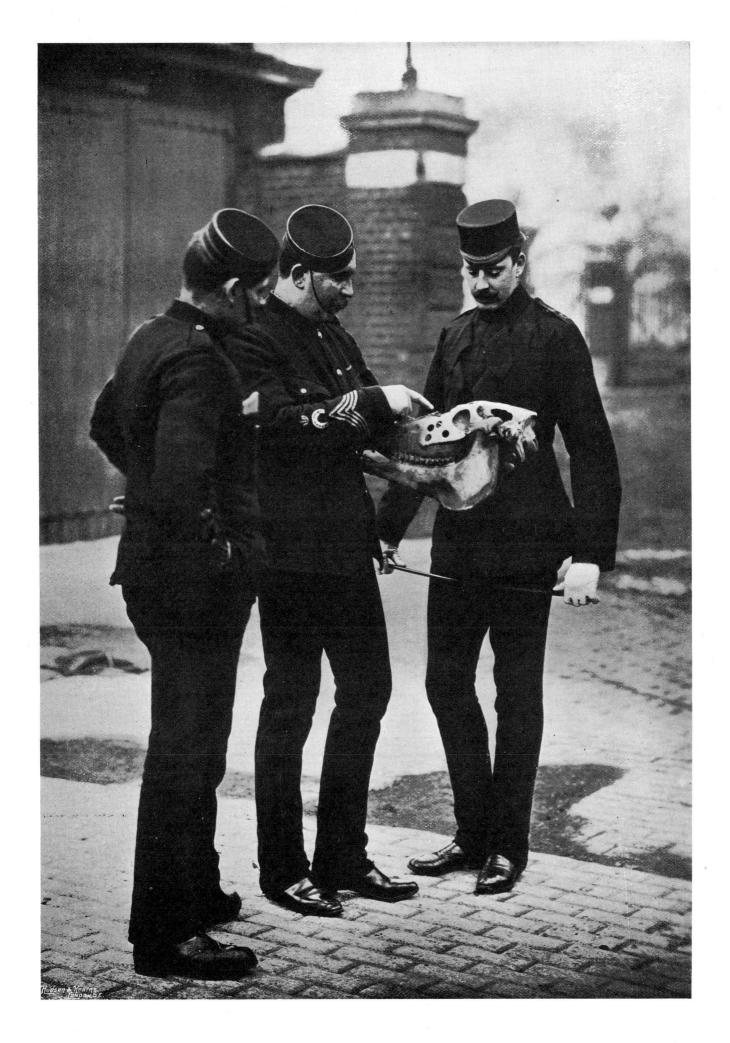

The Gloucesters at bayonet drill. The Gloucesters added to an
already illustrious record by a remarkable action in Korea in
1951—a police action for the U.N. Here they look like police.

The officers of the 'Queen's Westminsters'

In its officers, the 'Queen's Westminsters' is one of the most
favoured of Volunteer Corps. The rolls contain many names that
are widely known, and held in high consideration—two
Grosvenors, a Major and a Second Lieutenant; two Comerfords,
one the Lieutenant-Colonel and the other a Lieutenant;
a Trollope, the senior Major; a De Castro; a Stephenson, two
Roses, two Probyns; a Loder; a Canning; a Lambert. Every officer
under field rank has graduated at the School of Instruction and
bears the 'P.S.' after his name in the official Army List. The Colonel
of the Corps is the Duke of Westminster, and the Adjutant is
Major Hubert Leigh of the 'King's Royal Rifle Corps.'

Distinguished though their names may be, the officers of this
famous volunteer regiment look somewhat less than soldierly here.

44

'Where I dines I sleeps.' These straw palliasses will flatten with use. Usually they had a roughly triangular shape.

45

An ammunition mule of the 2nd East Lancashire Regiment
The British infantry soldier on the Home Establishment is allotted
on mobilization 185 rounds of rifle ammunition each man, which
is carried – 100 rounds by the man himself, 65 rounds as 'battalion
reserve' on mules and small arms ammunition carts, and 20 rounds
in the battalion baggage wagons. The mules, two in number to
each battalion, would find special employment in the field, and
among their duties would be to supply the fighting troops in
action with ammunition in connection with the battalion
small-arms ammunition carts (four in number per battalion)
posted in rear under shelter, by bringing up supplies as needed
in boxes (two per mule) each containing 1,100 cartridges and
weighing 75 lbs 10 ozs. Here we see one of the ammunition
mules belonging to the 2nd East Lancashire Regiment stationed
at Aldershot, with the men in charge.

The health and care of the mule was vital to the efficiency of the
regiment. The soldier on the left clearly has views on lack of
discipline and a proper sense of respect among mules; the man
on the right has given up the struggle.

Sergeants of the 18th and 73rd Field Batteries, R.A.

Nothing wrong with the ration scale here. Nevertheless, these sample
waistlines would not prevent their owners from setting a good
example under harsh physical conditions.

Above

In the Regimental cook house of the 3rd Dragoon Guards
Here we see the interior of the regimental cook house where all
the meals of the men, not married nor members of the sergeants'
mess are prepared. Each of the four squadrons of the regiment
selects two men as cooks, who are relieved of all regimental
duties except the annual musketry course. As a special inducement
to the satisfactory performance of the kitchen work a monthly
money prize is given to the cook who prepared the best dinners
in regard to cooking, serving, and making the most of the
materials. The cook house of the 3rd Dragoon Guards is in the
charge of Cook-Sergeant Albut, a soldier of 17 years' service and
a certified graduate of the Aldershot School of Cookery.

Above

In the saddle-tree makers' shop of the 3rd Dragoon Guards
This is a most important department in a cavalry regimental establishment, for everything connected with the accurate fitting and repairing of the saddle-trees for the regiment is seen to here. Nothing causes sore backs in horses more than ill-fitting saddle-trees, and the responsibility of the non-commissioned officer in charge of the department, the regimental saddle-tree maker, is no light one. The saddle-tree maker of the 3rd Dragoon Guards, Sergeant Smith—a veteran of 29 years' service—is here shown (in the centre of the foreground, wearing a white apron over a dark jacket). Round the room are sporting trophies shot in South Africa by two officers of the regiment.

Left

Indicted before a barrack room court martial
The unfortunate trooper of the Blues, who is seen in his shirt sleeves arraigned before his barrack room judges, opposite a sentry on temporary duty as well as a prospective executioner, may or may not get off lightly according to circumstances. If an old offender against barrack room law, he may be sentenced by the President of the Court—seated on the table with his helmet on—to anything from being tossed in a blanket to a ducking in the horse trough, possibly, even the headsman's axe:—to which *ultima ratio*, the jurisdiction of the Court extends.

This somewhat bewildering picture shows the lighter side of an aspect of community law. The offender might have stolen from a fellow soldier or told tales; if so, his punishment would be considerably less jolly than this. Soldiers usually preferred their own justice in such matters to official punishments.

49

Putting together a Berthon boat pontoon

Under Canvas during manoeuvres: *dinner-time*

Opposite

The Berthon Collapsible Boat was invented by a clergyman whose name the boat bears. It has now for military purposes been adapted for use with cavalry and flying columns as a light and easily carried pontoon. When so used, as our illustration shows, skids are placed across the thwarts of two boats (or the two halves of one boat), forming a platform or raft on which a gun or boxes of ammunition can be safely borne. The boat itself fits on a light cart, and can be taken anywhere, while a small-sized Berthon, able to float half-a-dozen men, can even be carried on a pack saddle. In the lower photograph we see an everyday incident of camp life, the cooks of a battalion — in the present case the 2nd Battalion Scots Guards — getting ready the men's dinners on the return of the troops to camp after a busy field-day.

Above

A Limber Ladder Bridge

The bridging operations represented here form part of the course of instruction in field fortification. The public generally understand by fortifications, permanent works, such as fortresses and coast batteries. These buildings are entrusted to the corps of Royal Engineers. Field fortification, on the other hand, must be known and practised by all arms, as it enables them to throw up hasty defences, and to move across streams and other hindrances that they may encounter in the field. Trestles, planks, spars, rope, casks, boats, and, in fact, anything available for the purpose, may be used in the construction of one or another kind of military bridge. The method of construction, the use of materials, and the duties of each member of the party are taught by an instructor, who sees that the work is practically carried out by the cadets themselves. Experience of soldiers' duties, not only by being drilled as privates in company and battalion, but by performing their manual labour, is one of the best qualifications for command.

At least they have the confidence to sit on their own handiwork.

Camp Life: *getting water*

Presumably an unofficial picture. Any C.O. would go audibly mad at seeing the mess around the tap. The lid appears still to be on the dixie and the water to be pouring down the sides!

Opposite
A soldier's kit inspection

Old soldiers often acquired a duplicate kit which was brought out for inspection only. Kit inspection did not usually include rifles; these were inspected on parade. Boots and leather were polished to a mirror-like finish and shirts were ironed flat and often sewn on the underside of the creases. However, when 'old soldiers' tricks' were made impossible, kit could still be brought to perfection by endless 'bull'. It kept men occupied, but not over-active, in hot, boring stations.

A Troop Stable: *16th Lancers*

Christmas Dinner Table: *16th Lancers*

The Soldier's Christmas Dinner.

Tommy was pretty keen. He even wears his tunic and medals for
Christmas Dinner.

Opposite

In a cavalry regiment Christmas is not so free from work—at least
in the morning—as in the infantry. Soon after Reveille the trooper
must be at 'stables', where he spends an hour or more attending
to his horse and accoutrements, nor is he at liberty to sit down
to breakfast until his horse has been fed. After breakfast he is
occupied in preparing for Church Parade, which usually takes
place about ten o'clock, and considering the extra equipment
carried by the average horse soldier in the way of cross-belt,
gauntlets and sword, the task is not to be completed in a few
minutes. At no time in the year is Church Parade witnessed by
such a vast concourse of the civilian population, who prefer
attending the Garrison Church, where they can hear the time-
honoured 'Adeste Fideles' and other Christmas hymns effectively
accompanied by the band. After church the feast of the day takes
place, laid out in a most lavish way, as we see it in the second
photograph. In decorating the barrack rooms, cavalry have the
advantage of being able to use curb-chains, swords, hoof-picks,
sheep-skins, and various pieces of horse furniture and equipment.
The lances, especially with pennon attached, standing out from
the walls, greatly add to the general appearance of the rooms.

These two pictures illustrate the ethos of the crack regiment.
Everything must be done in the right way in the right order.

Hudson & Kearns.
LONDON, S.E.

Above
Liquid provisions
This is a scene often witnessed in barracks, especially at Christmas time when Tommy Atkins takes the opportunity, after the good old English fashion, of making merry with his friends (and to make merry, Tommy must have beer, and plenty of it). The canteen authorities know that at such a universally festive season they must cater to the wishes of the rank and file, and accordingly an extra supply of beer and stout is ordered to the joy, not only of the contractor, but of those who patronise the canteen. That the load, on this occasion, is a heavy one, may be inferred from the size of the dray and the powerful horses. The duty of supplying malt liquors by contract to a regiment is only greatly sought after, for notwithstanding the work of 'The Army Temperance' and other kindred associations, all soldiers are not teetotallers, and, especially at the present season of the year, many are staunch supporters of 'Mr. Bung', provided the latter supplies them with desirable liquor.

Opposite
'No Fatigue Duties for Me.' *A Regimental Shoe-maker*
This illustration represents a trooper of the 3rd Hussars plying his trade as shoe-maker. Each regiment mends its own boots, and the shoe-makers not only are forgiven fatigue duties, but also earn extra pay.

Not well cleared

Preparing for the Royal Military Tournament. The camera sees
too much.

Above

The Hurdle Race
This photograph was taken at the sports at the Duke of York's
School, Dover. The hurdles are, as was usual at this time, wattle
fencing hurdles; technique is noticeably absent, and the judge
(holding on to his hat) seems to be a faster mover than the
competitors.

Opposite

**Physical training in the Army—A test of endurance on the
parallel bars**
In each large garrison there is a gymnasium, under a
superintendent, with a staff of non-commissioned officers as
instructors. All young officers and recruits have to go through a
gymnastic course on joining their battalions. There are also
courses for drilled soldiers, attendance for men under thirty years
of age being compulsory. For those who care for gymnastics there
are voluntary courses. At these one finds the very pick of Army
athletes—men who are seen at the Tournament and other
competitions.

Sword *v.* Sword

Sword *v.* Sword

That under ordinary conditions the lance, as a rule, has the advantage over the sword in combat seems to be now generally admitted among military experts. So much so, indeed, in our own Service that within the last few weeks, at the request of their colonels, steps are being taken to re-arm certain of our Bengal cavalry regiments, hitherto armed only with the sword, with the lance as well—at any rate, for the front rank men of squadrons. Four of our dragoon regiments also, during the last few years, have been given lances. The sword, however, has some chances of its own, more particularly in single combat, where the lance—essentially the weapon for 'shock-tactics' and to be used in attacks en masse—is apt to prove unwieldy against an active opponent who can get an attack home on the lancer's right side.

The formality of these pictures gives little hint of the skills involved. It took two years to train an efficient lancer.

Sword *v.* Lance: *A hit for the lance*

Sword *v.* Lance: *A hit for the sword*

Sports at Sandhurst in 1898

In view of the starting postures and clothing, it is remarkable that the race was won in the goodish time (on grass) of 2.2 minutes. The high jump was won at 5 ft 6 in. The average height of cadets was 5 ft 7 in.

Opposite

The art of boxing: *A set-to at Aldershot Military Gymnasium.*
These are a series of photographs taken at a Boxing Display at Aldershot Gymnasium, in which Captain Edgeworth-Johnstone took a prominent part. Tom Burrows, who is also shown here, has for a long time past been a civilian Athletic and Boxing Instructor at Aldershot Military Gymnasium. He is an Australian by birth, a genial and popular fellow, and Aldershot greatly regrets his recent departure to Cairo, whither he has gone to take up the post of Instructor to the Soldiers' Club. The hits shown in our photographs are these: (1) left-hand 'Hook Hit' on jaw (delivered on an adversary making a left-hand lead off at the head); (2) 'Side Slip' (to avoid an adversary's rush and left-hand lead); (3) 'Right-hand Cross Counter' on the angle of the jaw, a 'Knock-Out blow,' delivered on an adversary's left-hand lead; (4) 'Knocked Out,' a self-explanatory hit; (5) the large picture—right-hand 'Time' under chin, also delivered on an adversary's left-hand lead.

These pictures are clearly so contrived that they must have caused laughter even in 1890. In the bottom picture Burrows has obligingly dropped his guard and bent his head back as to be sure of receiving the blow on the Adam's apple—where it could prove near-lethal.

Left-hand 'Hook-Hit' on jaw

'Side slip'

'Right-hand Cross Counter'

'Knocked out'

Right-hand 'Time' under chin

Driver Welsh *v.* Corporal Merckel

Sapper Miles *v.* Private Regan

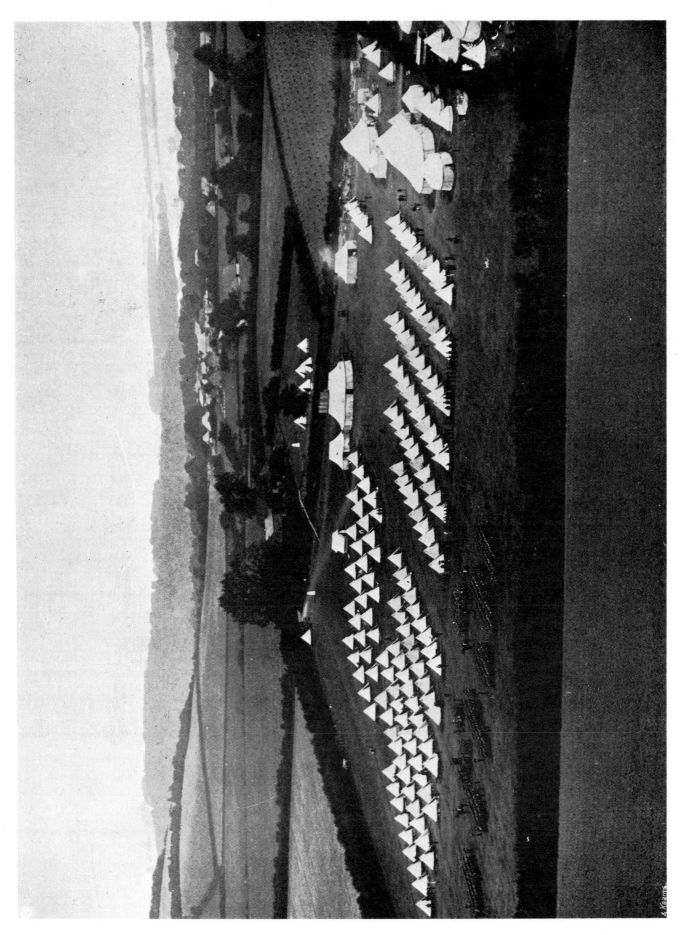

A Volunteer Camp—
before the days of air attack, when neat rows and white tents
made an easy target.

Above

The Staff of the Royal Military Academy

The present holder of the appointment of Secretary and Assistant Commandant is Lieutenant-Colonel F. A. Yorke, R.A., who occupies the same post which his father, General Yorke, held up to 1866 as Second Commandant and Director of Studies. A few changes have taken place in the personnel of the Staff, as shown in the illustration. The officer in the middle of the group is Lieutenant-General Sir William Stirling, K.C.B., who has been succeeded by General Hewett as Governor, with Colonel J. Murray, R.A., who was Colonel Yorke's immediate predecessor, on his left. It will be noticed that the civilian element forms no inconsiderable portion of the instructional staff. Sergeant-Major C. Gray, R.A., is the head of the warrant and non-commissioned officers attached to the Academy, and joined as a sergeant-instructor in 1880.

The Staff of the Royal Military Academy, Woolwich. In June 1896. The R.M.A. Woolwich, long known as 'The Shop', though nobody can explain why, was amalgamated with the R.M.C. Sandhurst in 1947, forming the present R.M.A. Sandhurst. 'The Shop' was founded in 1741. The R.M.A. had been established to provide trained officers for the new Royal Regiment of Artillery. Later it was extended to other technical arms. One of its more distinguished professors was Faraday (whose magnet is on show in the 'Faraday Hall'—a science block—at Sandhurst). An accompanying article gives the following information about R.M.A. life. 'Towards the close of the last century the regulations as to the manner of wearing hair were not only elaborate but severe. It was to be combed back with powder and pomatum and tied in a queue, and those gentlemen whose length of hair did not admit of this were to endeavour to promote the growth of it as much as possible, under penalty of degradation. In 1810 a dancing master was found necessary at a salary of £90 a year; a charge which we imagine would be as little to the taste of the modern taxpayer as the hair dressing then in force would be to the cadet of the present day.

The following may be taken as an example of the average daily routine at the R.M.A.—Reveillé sounds at 6.15 a.m. and defaulters are drilled from 6.30–7.00. The breakfast hour is 7.15. 8.15 to 9.45 is occupied by 'first study'. There is an interval of a quarter of an hour between the first and second study for all cadets except those whose presence is required in the orderly room, where offences are dealt with. Second study lasts from 10.00 to 11.45 as a general rule but in certain cases of practical outdoor work is prolonged to 1 or sometimes to 3 p.m. Lunch is at 1.15 while at 2.00 and 1.10 parades are held for riding and company drill according to class. The interval between 3.15 and 5.15 is free except for those studying languages or landscape drawing. A substantial afternoon tea known as 'Coffee Lunch' is on the hall table from 4.45 to 5.15 p.m. and there is a third study of two hours' duration from 5.15 to 7.15. Roll call is at 10.30.'

The Royal Military Academy Cricket Team, 1895
The half-page illustration represents the Cricket Team of 1895 with
the adjutant, Captain A. Handley, R.A., an Officer who is most
indefatigable as a coach in every branch of sport.

Hudson & Kearns London S.E.

Photo by W. M. Crockett, Plymouth.

Above

The 2nd Devons who appear here would all have retired by 1918, when the battalion was wiped out in a desperate and vital defence of the Aisne crossing. It was one of the most heroic actions of World War I, for they fought to the end with no hope of relief and saved the general situation.

Opposite, top

Musketry Drill in Barracks with the Coldstream Guards

Before the soldier goes to the ranges for rifle practice he is carefully instructed in the barrack square in everything that can possibly help forward his musketry training. To teach the elements of marksmanship, and train the arm, hand and eye to act together, an all-important preliminary, requires unremitting supervision and constant drilling. These men of the Coldstream Guards are under instruction in volley firing practice—with a view later on to the butts at Pirbright, and regimental work in the Long Valley during the Aldershot drill season.

Opposite, bottom

A Squad of the Coldstream Guards at Physical Drill

Physical drill is a comparative innovation in our Service, and owes its introduction, in the first instance, to the short-service system, and the urgent necessity for 'licking into shape' the young and immature recruits who nowadays find their way into the Army. These men belong to the Coldstream Guards, in their white undress jackets—a relic of the old white waistcoat that down to the days of William the Fourth every British soldier wore under his tunic.

Old soldiers may perhaps wonder how many hours of rehearsal preceded these 'informal' pictures.

Hudson & Kearns, LONDON S.E.

Photo by W. Gregory 4° Strand.

Hudson & Kearns, LONDON S.E.

Photo by W. Gregory 4° Strand.

The late P.M.O. and the Officers of the Staff

The Officers shown in the upper photograph are Surgeon-Major-General Charles Herve Giraud, Brigade Surgeon-Lieutenant-Colonel Blennerhasset and Surgeon-Major Pope. Surgeon-Major-General Charles Herve Giraud, A.M.S., in the centre of the group, has just handed over his charge as Principal Medical Officer at Netley. He has had an exceptionally distinguished career. Entering H.M. Service as Assistant-Surgeon on 10 March 1858, he saw service in the Indian Mutiny. We next find him engaged in the China War of 1860. He also took part in the expedition against the Taeping rebels, 1863–4, and was engaged in the South African Campaign of 1879–81. He has had charge of the Royal Victoria Hospital for the past two years, where, in a position demanding the highest administrative abilities, he has won golden opinions. Brigade Surgeon-Lieutenant-Colonel Blennerhasset, the officer shown on the left, performs the duties of secretary, and as 'registrar' is responsible for the statistical work of the establishment. He is also commanding officer of the 4th and 5th Companies of the Medical Staff Corps. Brigade Surgeon-Lieutenant-Colonel Blennerhasset was engaged in the late Ashanti Expedition, receiving a C.M.G. for his services. Surgeon-Major Pope, whose portrait appears on the right, is the adjutant of the Medical Staff Corps at Netley. This officer saw service in the Egyptian Campaign of 1882, and was present at the battle of Tel-el-Kebir. He was also engaged in the operations in Zululand in 1888.

The Senior Staff at Netley. Netley, 'the finest military hospital in the world', was the result of the outcry over hospital conditions in the Army at large and in Scutari, in 1855, in particular.

Opposite, bottom
In the lower picture Surgeon-Major Notter, M.D., Professor of Military Hygiene, is seen lecturing to the students in the Army Medical School. The staff of the school consists of four professors, four assistant professors, and a secretary.

The Nursing Sisters of the hospital

In the lecturing hall

Hudson & Kearns.

A convalescent

Our military hospitals are veritable models of cleanliness and comfort, but despite this fact, the majority of soldiers do all in their power to avoid being admitted as patients. They will suffer pain, attempt to 'doctor' themselves or even have recourse to quacks and quackery, but unless absolutely unfit for duty they refrain from placing themselves officially on the 'sick-list'. 'Tommy' is a bird of freedom, and he objects strongly to being obliged to lie on a bed of sickness for a term of weeks or months, but there are, at times, cases in which, owing to the severity of the ailment, his residence in hospital is rendered imperative. After weeks of pain, perhaps between life and death, one can well imagine how his heart is filled with gratitude to those, whose unremitting care and attention has succeeded in bringing him to a state of convalescence. Our illustration depicts a scene at the Herbert Hospital, Woolwich. The patient, attended by a nursing sister and two orderlies of the Medical Staff Corps, is enjoying in a bath-chair the open air, of which he has for a period been deprived.

Romance under inter-service conditions

ARMY CLOTHING

By

A Retired Officer of the Royal Army Clothing Department

[This Article is unsigned partly because it is necessarily, to some extent, a composite production, and partly because the gentleman responsible for the more important statements involved has private reasons for desiring to remain anonymous. The information, however, particularly as regards the Royal Army Clothing Department, is of a highly authoritative character, and as much of it has never before been published, the Proprietors of *The Navy and Army Illustrated* have decided to print it even without the added attraction of a signature.]

Since the clothing of the Army has been taken over by the public the soldier has derived great advantages, for not only has the quality been improved but a greater number of articles are now supplied, many of which, under the old system, had to be purchased by the soldier out of his own pocket. Thus in the old days when the Colonel supplied the clothing a cavalry soldier, in two years, obtained only two coats and one pair of overalls; now in the same period he gets from the public three coats, three pairs of overalls, two pairs of boots, two pairs of gloves, two forage caps and a pair of spurs. This represents an increase of pay of £1 10s. a year or 1d. a day.

The working of the Royal Army Clothing Department would necessarily appear rather complicated to the uninitiated mind, but in reality it has been reduced to a very perfect and reliable system. Some idea of the extent of this great establishment may be gathered from the fact that in addition to the work done for the Army, the Department makes issues to the Admiralty for Marines to India, for European troops, and to Colonial Governments, besides receiving and inspecting materials and articles of clothing for a dozen other services. Over 2,000 persons are employed, of whom about 1,500 are women. In engaging men preference is always given, when possible, to those who have served in the Army. The Department spends about a million and half sterling annually, and as a general rule makes about five-sevenths of the total clothing required for the Army in its own factory, about two-sevenths being given out to 'the trade'.

The annual cost of clothing a British soldier varies, of course, very considerably. Thus, the amount spent every year in making a Staff-Sergeant of the Royal Horse Guards the splendid object he is, approximates £14 10s., including a proportion of the cost of kit supplied on enlistment. In the case of an Infantry Private the amount is only three guineas, while in that of a Militia man it is only £1 6s. 3d. But in every case the supply is deemed fully adequate, and it must be remembered in this connection that the responsibility rests for quantity and pattern with the Adjutant-General's Department, and not with the civil side of the War Office. It is the Military authorities who settle what the soldier ought to have given to him and who seal the patterns of the various garments. The Royal Army Clothing Department then carries out the work, and the fact that the complaints from the Army are very few indeed in number, is sufficient proof that the supplies are satisfactory.

It is a little curious and indeed rather amusing that, notwithstanding the excellent results which have been attained under the present system, there should still exist in some military minds a conviction that the control of Army Clothing should be wholly in the hands of Army men. Officially speaking the whole matter has been threshed out, and a decision arrived at in favour of a continuance of civilian management; but there is still some sort of feeling on the point, and it is often asked if it would not be possible to place the Department altogether under, for instance, the Adjutant-General, instead of only giving the latter a right of inspection. Perhaps the best commentary on this aspect of the case is furnished by a humorous question once asked of an Adjutant-General by a former Director of Clothing, upon whom the Adjutant-General was striving to impress the desirability of a change of system: 'Is the Army seriously prepared to undertake the management of a factory where there are 1,500 women workers constantly employed, and, if so, how does it propose to go about it?' The story goes that this argument was conclusive, and that the spectacle conjured up of the Adjutant-General having to put on one side his every-day Army business in order to marshal and manage this tremendous array of female labour was altogether too terrible for actual contemplation. Speaking seriously, the main point to be borne in mind is that the control of a Department of this sort is in reality a commercial matter, and as such is far better left in civilian hands, so long as the Army gets what it wants as regards quality, number, and pattern.

One of the most important transactions ever carried out by the Army Clothing Department was the supply of clothing for the Egyptian Expedition of 1882. What had to be done at very short notice was to equip 11,000 Army Reserve men; to supply field kits for troops depatched from the Mediterranean, also helmets and climate clothing to troops sent from this country to the Mediterranean; to complete new clothing, white helmets, and field kits for about 23,000 men sent from this country; to provide and send from this country 25,000 additional suits of grey clothing with Bedford cord pantaloons, for the mounted troops, which had to be specially manufactured, together with such reserves as would keep the force in the field well supplied; to equip the Army of Occupation with tunics and winter clothing, also to re-equip the men returning from Egypt, and to provide plain clothes for men re-transferred to the Army Reserve. All this had to be done, and done quickly, and it was done, and done, moreover, satisfactorily. Nor, considering the magnitude of the operations, can the expenditure, which for clothing and necessaries in connection with the campaign amounted to under a quarter of a million, be deemed in any way excessive. But the main thing to be considered is, that this Expedition was a genuine test of our capacity to meet much more serious contingencies, and the fact that a test, in many respects a particularly searching one, should have been undergone without revealing any defects worth mentioning, is a striking indication of the improvements that have taken place in our position since the terrible days of the Crimean War. Before leaving this part of the subject it may be well to remark that, prior to 1878, there were no reserves of clothing, but in that year Lord Cranbrook authorised an expenditure of £200,000 to provide reserves of clothing and necessaries sufficient to equip one Army Corps of about 60,000 men, and this reserve has recently been increased, so as to supply clothing to all the First Class Army Reserve, numbering 85,000 men.

Of course, it will be understood that clothing is not supplied direct from the Pimlico factory to the back of the soldier. If it were it is greatly to be feared that the smart 'jacket' of the Royal Horse Artilleryman would not fit him by any means so beautifully as it generally does, and that the nether garments of the average trooper would be even less becoming than the baggy continuations of the French infantryman. The system in force provides for these risks by furnishing each corps with a sergeant master-tailor, a qualified tradesman, who has a regimental 'shop' in which he employs soldiers from the ranks as assistants, giving them a suitable addition to their pay. At stated intervals the men of the corps are measured for new clothes, and size rolls are made out and sent to the Pimlico factory, which is thus able to judge approximately what the demand for any particular corps is. The clothing is then issued in sizes as required to the corps, and the master-tailor fits the garments on each soldier in the presence of the officer commanding the unit to which the man belongs. In many cases the master-tailor is a very skilful cutter, and it is a tribute to the good quality of the cloth supplied that officers not unfrequently purchase Government serge and have it made up by the master-tailor for garments likely to undergo specially hard wear.

In India an allowance is issued to each soldier on which he is required to keep up a certain number of suits of American drill dyed, for active service and fatigue duties, to the well-known 'Khaki' or dust colour, in which some very excellent shades have been arrived at by means of really 'fast' dyes. When 'Khaki' was first introduced the fugitive nature of the dyes employed caused a great deal of trouble and produced occasionally some very comical results. Thus a battalion on parade might look very fairly well and extremely business-like in newly-dyed and newly-supplied Khaki uniform. But a week afterwards, when that set of clothes had gone to and returned from the 'dhobi' or washerman, the battalion would present an exceedingly variegated appearance, very detri-mental to the appearance of even the smartest corps, but simply unavoidable owing to the different action of the water upon different suits.

It is satisfactory that although 'Khaki' may be excellent for active service there is no tendency observable in any influential quarter to discontinue the use of red as the colour of the infantry soldier's tunic. The 'thin red line' is, of itself, such a glorious feature of our annals that any attempt to destroy this little bit of genuine 'local colour' would surely be disastrous. It is more than satisfactory, too, that a recent Act of Parliament has rendered it possible to punish those who wilfully bring Her Majesty's uniform into contempt. It is, no doubt, a compliment to the attractiveness of the said uniform that it should have been so extensively used for purposes of advertisement; but a line must be drawn somewhere, and Parliament has done well to draw it at sandwichmen masquerading as Field-Marshals and other similar vagaries calculated to distress the Army and lessen a soldier's honest pride in his habiliments.

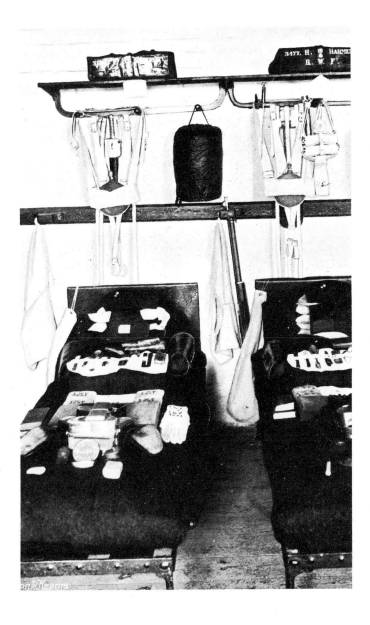

THE SOLDIER AT PLAY

By Callum Beg

Author of Our Citizen Army, The Life of a Soldier, etc.

All questions of military organization and reform are this year specially interesting. Great Britain has at length realized that her small Army is inadequate for the protection of the Empire. Parliament has lately sanctioned an increase of men in our land forces. The representatives of the people in the House of Commons have voted in favour of numerous measures for the benefit of the private soldier. A scheme for augmenting the artillery has been devised. All these are but signs of the times assuring as they are real. National sentiment is not dead. Patriotism will live as long as the British name endures. Despite this, the question of recruiting is always before us.

'Where are the men to come from?' many critics have asked. The question is a pertinent one. The young men of the nation are never behindhand when the voice of war is heard, but in time of peace comparatively few offer themselves for service under the Union Jack. There are doubtless many reasons to account for their want of eagerness. Chief among these may, perhaps, be placed ignorance, not only regarding the work of a soldier, but more especially on the subject of his recreation. A private is afforded greater facilities for recreation than are most of his friends in other walks of life. He has more time at his disposal, and can join in a game or witness an entertainment at a merely nominal price.

Recreation may be divided into two classes–active and passive. To the first belongs every species of sport or game. The second includes all ways of passing the time without bringing the muscles into play.

As a rule a man employed in any trade or calling has his fixed hours for work. The soldier, however, can never say with certainty when he will be at leisure. Today he may be a free man at midday. Tomorrow a route march and field day combined may furnish him with employment from seven in the morning till four in the afternoon. Such is the uncertainty of 'soldiering'; but, generally speaking, it may be fairly assumed that at 3 p.m. 'Tommy' is at liberty. Thus at every season of the year he can devote at least one hour to sport in the open air.

Among all games, football takes first place with the rank and file. In the eyes of 'Tommy' it is the sport of kings. An inter-regimental match is capable of transforming the most lethargic of soldiers into an excited individual hardly responsible for his actions. Should the contest be for the Army Cup, the interest evinced by all ranks is doubled. Indeed, it is doubtful if sudden and unexpected orders to 'embark for the front' would so much upset the usual tranquillity in barracks. For days before the event all other subjects of conversation are practically tabooed in the barrack-room, and the chances of victory are freely discussed. When the day fixed for the match arrives, few but those who are confined to barracks fail to witness the event, and ere the game has well begun the field is a veritable pandemonium, so loud are the cheers of the onlookers.

After the victory has been won the applause of the successful regiment knows no bounds. The air re-echoes with cheers for the winning team, and the victors are often carried to barracks shoulder-high. Despite all this display of regimental feeling, 'Tommy' is a lover of fair play. Notwithstanding the eulogy which he bestows on his comrades, he is sportsman enough to raise three cheers for the vanquished, provided, of course, that nothing has happened to cause 'bad blood'.

Each battalion or regiment has its team composed of the 'crack' players, but company and squadron teams are also formed and encouraged. They furnish befitting schools for young aspirants, who in time are drafted to the regimental team. It is natural, therefore, that matches between squadrons or companies are events second only in importance to inter-regimental contests. When the men of 'B' and 'C' Companies of, let us say, the Northern Light Infantry meet each other in the field, the event creates as much excitement among the two units concerned as that which pervades the whole battalion in the case of a match with the Wessex Fusiliers.

The men of each company appear in force to encourage their comrades, and, excepting the inferiority of play, the match might be one of much greater importance, so eager are the supporters of the rival teams. The regimental team is usually present in greater or less force to witness the form of the 'saplings', with a view to the acquiring of 'new blood'. Frequently, too, a company is captained by a man who plays for the regiment, and takes a pride in bringing his team to perfection. He is in a position to see the 'form' of his men, and to judge of their fitness for the regimental team. Though chosen to represent his regiment, he remembers the importance of company teams, and does all in his power to foster rivalry. If he be an officer as well he can make his influence doubly felt among the men. In almost every regiment officers are to be found playing both for their regiment and the company to which they belong.

Such a fact is sufficient to show that in the British Army, at least, there is a satisfactory understanding between officers and men. Far from proving derogatory to discipline, the mixing of officers and men in manly sports tends to bind all ranks more closely together. Nor are the regiments in which the officers hold aloof in this respect characterized by better behaviour. Too much cannot be said in favour of such a manly game. It develops the muscles, sharpens the wits, and, above all things, teaches the player self-restraint.

Cricket is, for the most part, in summer what football is in winter, although in some Scottish regiments it is practically impossible to form a team. The game is little played north of the Tweed, and, strange as it may seem, it is not unusual at Aldershot to find Scotsmen and North Countrymen indulging in an energetic game of football when the thermometer registers eighty in the shade. No wonder that men who play the game all the year can render such a good account of themselves.

As for football, there are regimental and company cricket teams. These are usually characterized by a good percentage of officers, who not only help the eleven to win, but contribute largely to the finances.

Apart from the physical aspect, there are undoubted advantages to be gained by taking part in either of the two great British games. Frequently the men of the regimental team are granted leave from parade either for practice or to admit of their playing a match. When this takes place at a distance, their railway fare is paid, and they have the advantage of a day's 'outing' and a change of air. So well is the financial side of the question arranged that the cost to the soldier is practically *nil*.

In every company or squadron there is an Amusement Fund, to which each man contributes the small sum of 3d. per month. Of this a certain percentage agreed upon is paid to the regimental team for its maintenance. The remainder is credited to the company, to be used in its own amusements, according to the wish of the majority. Needless to say, by far the greater portion is expended on football in winter and on cricket in summer. If the company be a strong one, the small charge is sufficient, together with donations from the officers, to provide the company team with a suitable outfit, and yet to leave a surplus available for other amusements.

The game of 'fives' is very popular with soldiers, especially at such places as Aldershot and Shorncliffe, where courts have been made for the purpose. Beyond the purchase of a ball the game involves little expense. The same may be said of 'rounders', to which soldiers, as a rule, are very partial. When a regiment is quartered either on the coast or near a river or canal, rowing forms one of the most attractive and healthy of pastimes. If the Amusement Fund be in a flourishing condition, each company can buy a boat for its own use, or at least hire one for the season.

This question is often intimately connected with the soldier's menu. There are stations in every part of Great Britain where fishing can be obtained without payment, and a company boat proves a useful adjunct in supplying the owners with a fish diet. At other places where the roads are good, bicycling naturally suggests itself to the soldier. In a company, one often finds three or four bicycles, provided partly out of the Amusement Fund and partly by subscriptions. The machines, being the property of the company, are kept under lock and key, and with the employment of a little tact on the part of the custodian, usually the colour-sergeant, there should be little dispute as to their being used.

Besides indulging in all outdoor sports, a soldier may, if he wish, attend the voluntary classes formed in every military gymnasium. Under qualified instructors, he has every opportunity of becoming proficient in all the regulation exercises, and of learning something of fencing, single-stick, and 'the noble art of self-defence'.

In the cavalry the practice of tent-pegging, heads and posts, etc., may well be classed under the head of sports.

In every branch of the Service athletic sports are held at least once a year, when a soldier is afforded an opportunity of entering into every species of manly contest.

So much for recreation of the first class; but that of the second must not be forgotten. Within the barrack walls the canteen, perhaps, affords the most popular form of amusement. It usually consists of a bar and large hall, furnished with numerous tables, and fitted with a stage. In the evening a variety entertainment is provided, generally graced by the presence on the stage of professional artistes. Soldiers form a most appreciative audience joining as they do in the chorus of every song. 'Tommy Atkins' regards the canteen as his own particular property, and rightly so. To witness the performance he need not array himself in 'walking-out dress'. He can buy his liquid refreshments at a reasonable price, and, being beyond the jurisdiction of the London County Council, is permitted to consume it in the auditorium.

Besides the canteen there are regimental coffee bars, recreation-rooms, and libraries. The first, usually attached to the second, retail all kinds of non-intoxicant liquors and eatables. The recreation-room is designed for billiards, bagatelle, dominoes, and the like, and for entertainments of various kinds. The library, well stocked with standard literature and newspapers, is the resort of the studious. Doubtless most civilians would be surprised to see how many soldiers support the institution, for the use of which and the recreation-room a man is charged 3d. per month.

Almost every regiment has its dramatic club or niggerminstrel troupe. Such dramatic and musical talent finds an outlet in entertainments given from time to time during the winter months.

In most garrison towns there are soldiers' homes, where soldiers may pass the time in many ways. These are excellent institutions, but their connection with one or other religious body renders them less popular with soldiers than they would otherwise be.

We have only ventured to touch upon the principal means of recreation which soldiers are enabled to enjoy; but our object is gained if we have enlightened even a few with regard to the amusements of 'Tommy Atkins'.

THE SOLDIER AS HE IS

By

Major-General H. M. Bengough, C.B.,
Commanding 1st Infantry Brigade, Aldershot

THE soldier as he is, and the soldier as he is popularly represented, are to say the least of it, two very different pictures.

It is, I think, commonly supposed, and the error is not confined to civilians, that the recruit when he puts on his soldier's coat, be it red or blue or green, puts off, so to speak, his humanity, and becomes forthwith a mere machine, sinking his individuality, and forfeiting his right to personal opinion.

Now in the case of the 'old soldier', that is the man with some 21 years' service and 5 good conduct badges, or 5 sheets in the defaulters' book, as the case may be, there may be some grounds for this belief. The heavy hand of discipline and the ceaseless round of routine, no doubt, tend to emasculate individuality, and create a being *sui generis* of a different growth to his fellow creatures. But the soldier we have now to deal with is enlisted as a lad, passes his boyhood, so to speak, in the ranks, and leaves the service at an age when his fellow citizens are but entering in a trade or profession.

But I have said that this mistake as to the characteristics of our soldiers extends to the Service itself. Few officers understand their men, not from want of interest in them, not even for lack of sympathy with them, but because tradition has handed them down as units in a machine, discouraging individuality, and almost forbidding them to act or think for themselves. Yet soldiers have their opinions now-a-days as have other folk, and, like that of other folk, a very varied opinion it will be found to be on most questions. 'Tot homines tot sententiæ' will be found as true in the ranks as in other paths of life, and very difficult it is to arrive at any general consensus of opinion among soldiers on a given question. Of course, be it understood that in matters of discipline no opinion can be asked, but there are many matters affecting the comfort and well-being of the man in which it may be well to know what they themselves think.

I remember some years ago organizing a novel experiment in India in the way of a rifle camp at some distance from the station under my command, to which the men were allowed to go on condition of their entering for the matches which were principally of a tactical nature. The camp was well attended, and I thought the experiment a success, but it being something of a new departure I was anxious to obtain the opinion of the men themselves on it, and accordingly I asked an old soldier, who had been assisting at the camp, whether the men liked it. His answer, not too encouraging, was 'Well, Sir, there's some of 'em does and some of 'em doesn't.' And this, as far as my experience goes, is about as near as you will get to unanimity on any question among any class of men.

At the same time, I think that many a useful hint can be obtained from soldiers on matters of dress and equipment on which they can speak with the best of all knowledge, that of practical experience.

But besides private opinion there is in the ranks a strong public opinion on many questions, and none the less strong because it is not given expression to.

I trust I may not be considered as cherishing a purely Utopian hope when I say I look to this public opinion among the rank and file as the means of removing entirely the one blot in our Army, the vice of drunkenness. This evil has greatly diminished of late years, a circumstance due no doubt to the spread of Temperance Societies, but it will not die out until the men themselves take it in hand, and it shall come to be considered quite as much of a disgrace for a private soldier to be drunk as it is now held to be for an officer. And we may not have very long to wait, for I can remember when I joined the Service an officer was thought rather a poor sort of fellow who did not, occasionally at least, exceed in his cups.

There are still many highly respectable old people, especially in the country districts of England who would look upon their own son 'listing as 'going to the dogs', and who regard any one in a red coat as one of the bold and dissolute soldiery of past centuries, or of the days of crimps and press-gangs. Much has been done to dispel this illusion and to place the British soldier in his true light by the manoeuvres that have been held in different parts of the country, and by the excellent practice of marching regiments through their territorial counties. The conduct of soldiers on these occasions has invariably been such as to call forth praise from all with whom they come in contact. During the late manoeuvres in the New Forest two divisions of Infantry besides Cavalry and Artillery, some 12,000 men in all, were encamped for some days in a private park and grounds in a country strictly preserved, and the owners stated that if asked to assess the damage done to their property they could not fairly rate it at higher than 5/–!

On what grounds, then, do the objections to allow a relation to 'go as a soldier' rest? In so far as they have any valid grounds they may be said to be fear of bad example and of unsettling a young fellow for regular work, and dislike of service abroad. There are of course a certain number of black sheep in every flock, and the Army is no exception, but they are a very small minority, and their life in the Service is generally a short one; and, as regards the second objection, I cannot see how habits of punctuality, respect to superiors, smartness and cleanliness and the endurance of certain hardships, can render any young man unfitted for the battle of life. As for the short term of foreign service that falls to the lot of a soldier, he should with ordinary care of himself, and the exercise of a little common sense, return to his home with a mind improved and enlarged, and a good sum in the Savings Bank.

Is the Service popular? I think so. Young soldiers are now treated with much consideration, they have excellent food, are not overworked, are comfortably housed and clothed, and what with excellent recreation rooms, and cricket and football and rifle clubs and other amusements, to say nothing of prospects of promotion and chances of distinguishing themselves on service, they are in a far better position than they could ever hope to be in any other profession open to their class in life.

Neither is the soldier's fate to be deplored, when his time comes to be ordered abroad. I have questioned many a young fellow under orders to join a draft proceeding to India, and they almost invariably look forward pleasurably to the idea of seeing a new country. And indeed there is much to be said in favour of a soldier's life in India. Besides the novelty of the change, things are in many ways made pleasant to him in the East. He has more leisure time, perhaps a little too much leisure for his good, a boy to clean his boots very often, though I don't myself approve of this luxury for soldiers, a cook who will not object to provide him with any little extra dish he may fancy, and if of a sporting turn he can take a gun and ramble almost where he will. There is, of course, another side to the picture in such trials as heat, mosquitoes, absence from friends, and the like; but what I think a soldier misses more abroad than anything else is his evening stroll in his garrison town, with its gas-lit streets, its bright shop windows, and gay music halls. These are the scenes in which he finds his chief delight, for he is easily amused, and though not possessed of that light-hearted southern disposition that enables a Spaniard to feel supremely happy with a cigarette, a glass of lemonade and a smile from a pretty girl, yet with his pipe and glass of beer and a pleasant word with the girl he loves, or thinks he loves, he passes his time in perfect content if not in exuberant happiness.

The Soldier in Action

The probable character of future wars is somewhat misty. It is impossible to foresee the effect which will be produced by the vast improvements that have been effected in the precision and rapidity of fire of modern weapons, both of Artillery and Infantry, since the last great European war. That it will bring a greater strain than ever on the nerves of those engaged may be accepted as certain. I do not think that we as a nation will be unfavourably affected as compared with other nations.

I have often thought that our army comprises in its mixed rules the best fighting characteristics of the most warlike nations in Europe. The Irish have the military instinct, the dash in action, the cheeriness in camp, and the good marching qualities of the French; the Scotch possess the long-headed, cool, almost methodical temperament and strong sense of discipline of the German soldier, whilst the English represent the dogged determination, the resolute refusal to acknowledge defeat, that characterise the Russian. It is qualities such as these that have extended the British Empire to the vast dimensions to which it has now attained, and it is on qualities such as these that we must rely to maintain that Empire intact. I believe that the British soldier of today will in the stress of trouble, if it comes, prove himself equal to the task.

Tommy Atkins

I have refrained from referring to the soldier by his now familiar soubriquet of Tommy Atkins. Although this cognomen has been, so to speak, immortalized in the pathetic and stirring stanzas of Rudyard Kipling, I doubt whether its application is altogether acceptable to the man. A soldier has a Briton's characteristic dislike to anything like ridicule, however kindly meant and aptly put, and I think that he suspects a latent slight, even in the friendly rhymes of the Soldier's Poet.

However this may be, I am sure that the soldier has a very sensitive nature, and is far more keenly alive to a word of rebuke or of praise than is generally imagined. Knowing this, as most officers doubtless do know, I have often wondered that greater advantage is not taken of it as a lever to good conduct and to smartness in the performance of duty. A word or two of commendation for instance from an officer to a soldier on parade or on a field day, would not only please the man himself and encourage him to renewed exertions, but it would put him at once a head and shoulder above his comrades. I can remember more than one instance in which a few words of praise thus bestowed have been remembered years after the event. It is, moreover, by such means that a soldier's affection is gained, and that gained he is capable of any deed of self-sacrifice.

And this leads me to remark on the keen sense by which a soldier detects anything in his superiors that seems to show a want of good breeding. A true gentleman secures his willing obedience. It is not the surface gentleman who succeeds in securing his respect. The soldier has an instinctive faculty for looking in these matters below the surface and recognizing the kindly heart, no matter what the exterior. I know that a

soldier will work more willingly for one whom he likes, even though he may now and then let drop a rough word, than for one with a smooth tongue but a lack of sympathy.

Another salient characteristic in the soldier is his aversion to any exceptional treatment as an individual, to anything that makes him a marked man, and this leads occasionally to somewhat curious developments. I may give an instance. It has been constantly the aim of officers interested in the well-being of their men to induce them to forego the old-established habit of drinking their beer at the Canteen at 12 o'clock, instead of with their dinners at 1 o'clock. Many a device has been tried to overcome this rather barbaric custom, but, I believe, invariably without success. Most of the plans have failed because they entailed extra trouble on some one. To meet this, and to reduce the labour to a minimum, I had a roll of a Company prepared and hung up in the barrack room, with columns in which a man had only to make a mark in a certain column opposite to his name to ensure having a pint of beer or bottle of ginger beer on the dinner table. I gave each man a tumbler, and had great hopes of success, as the officer to whom I entrusted the experiment took a keen interest in it, but I was doomed to disappointment. The plan did not 'take on'. Day after day it was reported to me that the columns remained unfilled. I was fairly puzzled, but at last it transpired that the reluctance of the men to fill in the columns arose from an objection to its being known whether or not they drank beer. Possibly they suspected a trap, and imagined that the beer drinkers would be branded as drunkards. Since then I have given up all idea of reforming the soldier in this respect: perhaps, after all, he is even in advance of his time, and has anticipated modern hygienic theories that food should be taken without liquid.

The soldier at Play

Football is the only game into which the soldier throws himself with any real zest. At cricket he is a 'dilettante', at football an enthusiast; and this passion is only of very recent development, being indeed synchronous with the keen public interest that has of late been evinced in this game.

It would be an interesting study, but one quite outside the scope of this article, to trace the causes that have given a game so rapid and decisive an ascendancy in the public estimation. I suppose there are twenty football clubs now to one that existed twenty years ago, and, if crowds of spectators are a test of comparative popularity, cricket simply isn't 'in it'. Whatever the cause, I, as a soldier, welcome the revival of the fine old English game heartily. There can be no better pastime for soldiers than football, combining as it does skill, judgment, pluck, resource, activity—all soldierly qualities—and affording amusement to all, from the recruit enjoying the humble punt-about in the parade ground to the crowds of enthusiasts keenly watching a hard contested struggle for the final ties for the Army Cup.

Space and time forbid me pursuing these rambling notes on a soldier's life. If they should serve, in however humble a degree, to awaken an interest in a servant of the State, whose one proud boast it is that he has always done his duty and is ready to do it again, I shall not think that my pen has been misemployed.

H. Bengough,
Major-General.

THE ADVANTAGES OF MARRYING A SOLDIER

By Cicely McDonnell

To describe the private soldier's wife as a *femme incomprise* would scarcely be an exaggeration; nothing is more difficult to educate than public opinion. From reading Lever and other novelists of years ago, the idea prevails that so soon as any self-willed girl enters the married state with a soldier, her life thereafter consists of a desperate struggle to make both ends meet. Surely nothing could be further from the fact than this notion. 'During fifteen years' experience,' said a non-commissioned officer recently, 'I have never once seen it justified'.

Though, unfortunately, some undesirable matches are contracted there, many well-educated, well-brought-up girls marry into the ranks, and bear the difficulties, anxieties, and sorrows that in some cases are the lot of a soldier's wife, with a courage and fortitude that do credit to themselves and all belonging to them.

The object of this article is not to show the women of the regiment in any fanciful light, but to describe as fully as possible the advantages they enjoy. As to social status, there is no doubt that the position of the average soldier's wife is infinitely superior to that of the wife of the civilian in receipt of an income of like value.

The advantages, as compared with those of the artisan or married man of any station lower than the middle class, are as follows: Sanitary dwellings, *no rent*, bright and cheerful surroundings, gas, coals, firewood, schooling for children free; the certainty of a fixed daily quantity of wholesome food; the provision of clothing of all kinds (so far as the husband is concerned), without the eternal necessity for painful calculations as to the means of procuring the wherewithal; the opportunity of purchasing everything necessary for housekeeping from the canteen, which is an institution arranged on purely socialistic principles, i.e., the men and women share the profits, which are distributed in kind; the annual change of air and scene; travelling expenses free, and facilities under certain conditions; and a certain, if small, income. Medical attendance and the services of the Army chaplains are always at the disposal of married couples without expense; and in case of the husband being detailed for duty at a distance, a separation allowance is made; that is, in the case of wives who are 'on the strength' of the regiment.

Above all, a soldier's wife is free from the wearing anxiety lest through strikes, business losses, reduction of staff, etc., her husband should lose his berth at short notice, and she should suddenly find herself in the direst straits through complete loss of means.

Further, a girl who marries either a 'trooper' or a 'private' realizes that her husband has chances of advancement, distinction, and reward, and that, as he rises, her position is improved, and she may become a person of some importance; and, again, a private soldier (if he avails himself of them) has opportunities of improving himself. From force of circumstances, he is thrown amongst very mixed companionship; but he is also in daily contact with men, as his officers, who have received the best of education, and whose manners he can study, whose bearing he can imitate. Example is better than precept, and the wife sometimes gains vicariously by this association, and, if she is intelligent, adapts herself quickly to the better side of barrack life, and finds the order and discipline regulating her ways too.

Looking at the subject from its most unfavourable aspect, should a young innocent girl marry a reprobate of the worst description, whose only recommendation has been the uniform he has been lucky enough to wear; should this man commit an offence of the most unpardonable kind, and accordingly be sent for a certain term to a military prison, the wife, in such case, will remain in her quarters provided by Government, will draw all her allowances, and receive at the hands of everyone around her the most sympathetic treatment. And, if there is any of the old Adam left in a man when he enlists, it can safely be assumed that no treatment is better adapted for knocking it out of him than the training of a soldier. So that although a woman might marry a villain, the Service will 'lick' him into shape for her better than any other system of which I am aware.

The consent of the commanding officer is necessary before getting married, but this would not be withheld unless the man were of notoriously bad or improvident character; and inquiries are usually made by the officer as to the character of the woman before giving sanction for marriage. In special cases, soldiers married without leave may be allowed to be out of mess, in order to contribute the better to the support of their families.

In case of the death of a soldier before the expiration of his period of Army service, his widow is entitled to claim all moneys, deferred pay, etc., standing to his credit. When a soldier is killed in action, or dies of wounds received in action within twelve months, his widow is granted a gratuity of one year's pay. In such cases gratuities are also granted to orphans.

The advantages granted to married soldiers by regulations are confined to those on the married roll. This contains all of the rank of sergeant, or above, and from 3 per cent in the infantry to 7 per cent in the Household Cavalry of the rank and file; while the Freemasonry that forms a brotherhood in the world at large is as nothing compared to that that binds together the members of a regiment. It is not exaggerating to say that nowhere else can be found such *esprit de corps*, such practical sympathy, such willingness to help others in debt or in trouble.

Every regiment, naturally, has its own rules and regulations as to the accommodation granted to married couples, as to married quarters and conveniences; but whatever the drawbacks may be, it cannot be denied that barracks are, as a rule, built in a fairly open position; therefore a soldier's wife does not experience the squalid, sordid surroundings that are the frequent condition of the artisan class—at all events, of many who live in crowded London, and many of the manufacturing towns.

To each married non-commissioned officer and private, rooms are allotted in proportion to rank, seniority, and size of family; and, so far as possible, any complaints as to accommodation, etc., are suitably listened to and remedied by the commanding officer. When quarters are changed, the out-going regiment is supposed to leave the quarters fit for occupation, and should it happen (as occasionally it does) that the rooms assigned to any married couple are really too dirty to be occupied, a small sum of money is given so that the necessary cleaning may be done.

When a regiment is ordered from one place to another, at any long distance, but not abroad, an allowance is made for moving expenses. It may be that some of the married couples have furniture they do not wish to sell, and cannot remove owing to the expense; in such case, the quartermaster arranges for a basement room or dry cellar in the barracks, and the pieces of furniture are labelled and warehoused, free of charge, until the return of the regiment, when a fatigue party is told off to collect, remove, and distribute them in the fresh quarters assigned to the owners. The usual term of residence in one place is twelve months.

As regards rations, bread is drawn twice a week by all. Staff-sergeants draw their meat twice a week, privates once. In some regiments the married privates receive a larger allowance of coal in winter per week than the non-commissioned officers, and a quartern more bread. Should a baby be born, the private's wife receives a present of 27s., where the non-commissioned officer's wife only gets 21s. These bonuses would be more than acceptable to many a City clerk on such occasions.

It is well known that married soldiers (as well as single) can add to their pay by taking over various duties, such as orderly clerkships, school-masterships, tailoring, 'instruction', etc., while the wives are frequently employed by the officers' families as house-helps, needle-women, dressmakers, and as laundresses.

Here, again, soldiers' wives are lucky, for the laundry arrangements are as complete as can be. It is not a case of doing the washing in their rooms, and thus rendering home a place of general discomfort. Washing, drying, and ironing rooms are provided, and some of the women earn as much as £2 a week, which they can receive either in the small payments or *en bloc* once a quarter. The mess linen is generally given out to the wives of time-expired or discharged men, so even they benefit by their connection with the Army.

The wives of the bandsmen are particularly lucky, for their husbands are allowed to accept private engagements to play at parties, etc., for which they each receive a fee of 18s. to 21s. generally; they may also take employment in theatre orchestras, provided they do not neglect their regimental duties. Some of the 'solo' bandsmen make very good incomes.

A special Government industry open to the women is the making of shirts for the Army, for which they receive payment at the rate of $8\frac{1}{2}$d. each—a large sum in proportion to that earned by many poor women and girls engaged in similar work in the East End. As regards the purchase of stores and groceries, these can be procured in the canteen at the most moderate prices; a large profit on the part of the management is not desired, the object being the benefit of the community, and the wages for service are a small item. Still there is a good profit, and, as the canteen fund is not allowed to exceed a certain sum, the surplus is divided in kind.

As regards social amusements, and so forth, soldiers' wives have plenty of opportunities of enjoyment, in the form of dances, concerts, sports, etc. It is not that they have to lay themselves out to obtain them as best they may, but that they are part of their life. How far the wives participate is decreed (as before) by the etiquette of the regiment into which they marry.

In the Household Cavalry there is a weekly dance in barracks, which the troopers' wives attend as a matter of course; then there is the annual ball, for which a room is hired, and to which the public are admitted by purchase of tickets. The officers and their wives attend these balls and dances, and they are very much enjoyed by all. In the Foot Guards only the non-commissioned officers' wives go to the dances, but the concerts and entertainments are open to all; while at Christmas the commanding officers pay for the Christmas dinner, and there is a special allowance made to married couples. The officers' wives give the children a Christmastree party; the colonel gives the non-commissioned officers, as a body, a dinner; and the wives go in afterwards.

When a regiment is ordered for foreign service, the wife has to face the fact that her little home must be broken up and the furniture sold. This, no doubt, seems very hard, but there are compensations in every lot. Women who, if married to clerks and mechanics, would never have a chance of leaving England now experience the pleasures of travel, and those who have been in India long heartily to go there again and enjoy the lazy sunny life. The voyage on the troop-ship is a new experience, and any discomfort of life on board is amply atoned for by the novelty of the situation. When the vessel touches at a port, permission is given to go on shore for a few hours. In India the non-commissioned officers' wives generally have two native servants, an ayah, and a 'boy'. There also the wife receives an allowance of 4 rupees a month for herself, and 2 rupees 8 annas for each child; this is absolutely her own to spend as she likes. The wives who are not on the strength can only follow the regiment at their own expense.

When a regiment is ordered for active service the crucial test has to be endured, viz., the separation of husband from wife, child, and home. Then the wife goes through a painful struggle between love and duty. The parting may mean parting for ever from the man she loves and may never see again; and she has to muster all her courage to enable her to bear up bravely at the last sad moment. During her husband's absence, he arranges for her to receive what is called the 'biggest-half' of his pay; in many cases she draws all, and he simply takes the extra allowance for field service himself. Should he, alas! be killed in action, she receives a gratuity both for herself and orphans, which helps and sustains her at the moment of her heaviest trial. Without trying to put a rosy haze on the subject, the foregoing facts show that a woman who marries a soldier has solid comforts that many civilians' wives lack. As regards her happiness in the state, or the comforts she obtains or surrounds herself with, that depends to a great extent on her temperament. A good manager will always make the best of things, a happy disposition finds happiness where others find misery and hardship. Our lives are much as we make them.

TYPES OF OUR ARMY

Drum Major, London Scottish

The London Scottish, founded 1839, were, and are, a volunteer
force.

Above

A gathering of the Clans

Of all the dumb pets in the Army, dogs always have been, and must still continue to be, the most numerous. Many of the officers of almost every regiment own one or two and sometimes more. In the picture are to be seen a number of the officers of the 1st Seaforth Highlanders and a dog for almost every officer—some with rough coats, some with smooth coats, big dogs, little dogs: all appear to have won the affection of their masters. These dogs usually travel with the regiment to which their master belongs, and in this connection may be mentioned the famous Bobbie of the 66th Regiment. This faithful creature went all through the Afghan Campaign, in which he was wounded and, when that regiment returned home, was decorated with the Afghan medal by Her Majesty at Osborne.

Opposite

'Second to none.'–*The Scots Greys*

The Scots Greys were originally the North British Dragoons, whose first Colonel was Graham, of Claverhouse. Their grey horses, the legend goes, were the gift of William the Third, for good service in Flanders. Their bearskins were won under Marlborough at Ramillies, where the Greys overthrew the famous French Regiment, du Roi. Twice since then have the Greys taken standards in battle: the white damask 'Giants' flag of the French Household Cavalry at Dettingen, and the eagle of the French, '45th of the Line' at Waterloo. In the charge of the Heavies at Balaclava they displayed splendid heroism. The Honorary Colonel of the Greys is the Czar of Russia, to whom recently the regiment sent congratulations on the birth of the Grand Duchess Olga.

The Scots Greys on parade. The regiment is now merged with the Carabiniers to become the Royal Scots Dragoon Guards.

Hudson & Kearns.
LONDON, S.C.

85

The White Donkey's Companion
The Sirdar [Kitchener] has presented to the Queen a large
Egyptian she donkey. It is of the same type as the male donkey
already owned by Her Majesty, but is white, instead of being
marked with grey like the male. The animal was shipped at Suez
in the 'Duke of Argyll'.

Either Kitchener or Queen Victoria lacked a sense of humour.

The Drum-Major and Goat of the 1st Battalion Welch Regiment
Sergeant-Drummer McKelvey has seen fourteen years' service in his regiment, which he joined at the age of eighteen. As he stands six feet high in his stockings he, moreover, makes, in the full dress of his rank, a very effective figure on parade and at the head of the battalion at a march past. The regimental goat is an important institution in all Cambrian Regiments and led by the Sergeant-Drummer (the modern official designation for the historic title of 'Drum-Major') appears at all parades at the head of the regiment. The goat seen in the photograph is a newcomer, and was taken on the strength of the battalion in the place of an old regimental favourite that died in August last on the day after the 1st Welch reached Plymouth, after having marched through Wales at the head of the corps. 'Gwell angau na Chywilydd' or, Anglicized, 'Better death than shame' is the proud motto of the regiment.

Sergeant

Pioneer-Corporal

Types of our army! These pictures were taken in Malta. They were meant to enhance the army's prestige in the eyes of the public.

Private

Bandsman

Orderly

Drummer

Above

The Veteran – improving the occasion
Here we see a Bugler of the Coldstream Guards utilizing an old
Chelsea pioneer – an ex-Guardsman and the bearer of war and good
service decorations – as an object lesson, as it were, for the benefit
of a younger comrade, a Drummer Boy of the Grenadiers. The
moral ought not to be a hard one to point, for good character is
the all important essential of the qualifications required of old
soldiers who are desirous of being enrolled among the five
hundred and odd in-pensioners at the Royal Hospital, Chelsea.
Preference is at all times given to those among the
out-pensioners of the institution (old pensioned soldiers), who
have borne the best characters and rendered the longest service,
and at the same time are unable to supplement their pensions
owing to loss of limbs, wounds and other injuries received on
service, or are incapable from other causes (if over fifty-five years
of age) of earning anything additional. The in-pensioners are
clothed, housed, fed and medically attended to at the expense of
the State, and receive a small allowance of pocket money in lieu
of their out-pension, which ceases on admission within the
walls of Chelsea.

Opposite

'Lizzie', the pet bear of the 17th Lancers
Of the many regimental pets in the Army not many, probably,
have a more interesting story attaching to them than the subject
of our illustration, 'Lizzie', of the 17th Lancers. Her mother was
shot in Cashmere, eight years ago, by Prince Adolphus of Teck,
who brought the cub to Lucknow, where the regiment was
stationed, and gave her as a present to his troop. Shortly after this
the cub was lost for a year. Then one day a man came round with
a performing bear, which was recognized as 'Lizzie'. Since then
'Lizzie' has remained with the 17th, with whom she came to
England in 1889. She is a great pet with all ranks, for her own
part reciprocating the affection, specially in favour of Corporal
Baker, her particular guardian, who is shown in the illustration.
'Lizzie' lives on bread and milk, jams, and fruits, and goes
every day to the canteen for a pint. She takes to water, and
enjoys a swim in the summer.

Hudson & Kearns,
London, S.E.

92

Hudson & Kearns.
London, S.E.

Opposite
Two Military Men of the Year
Few if any, of the readers of *The Navy and Army Illustrated* will
fail to recognize at a glance the two officers whose portraits we
give here. The tall officer in Life Guardsman's uniform is
Captain Oswald Ames, of the 2nd Life Guards, the tallest officer
in the British Army, who, at the Prince of Wales's special request,
was selected, together with four of the tallest troopers of his
regiment, the 2nd Life Guards, to form the escort to the bluejackets
who, with their guns, headed the Jubilee State Procession.
Captain Ames entered the Army in 1884, becoming captain in
1892. The other officer shown is Captain the Hon. Maurice Gifford,
of the Rhodesian Horse, who, as he rode among the Colonial
Contingent at the head of his smart-looking group of cavalrymen
in their khaki uniforms and 'smasher' hats, received a welcome
from all London that was in heartiness second to none.

Above
Two notable guardsmen
Second Lieutenant Heathcote-Amory of the 1st Battalion
Coldstream Guards, is the tallest officer (6 ft 5¼ in.) in the
Guards' Brigade. The drummer is John Marshall, a boy with a
story. Picked up at the manoeuvres near Swindon, in 1893, while
following the troops, and found to be an orphan and a fine
spirited boy, the officers of the battalion placed him in the
Gordon Boys' Home. There John Marshall did well and became
cornet player in the band, whence the officers of the Coldstream
Guards took him into their own band as a drummer. He is a
universal favourite and a good boy.

The Gordon Boys Home was founded by public subscription after
General Gordon's death at Khartoum.

Hudson & Kearns.

Above
20th Middlesex (The Artists)

The Artists Rifles. They acquired their name from the large number of famous painters and sculptors who served in their ranks. These included such notables as Millais, Leighton and Holman Hunt. The regiment was remarkably efficient (in those days artists prided themselves on being physically tough) and subsequently had a distinguished record in World Wars I and II, though mainly as an officer-producing unit. Today it is the 21st Special Air Service Regiment (Artists), one of the territorial battalions of the élite SAS regiment.

Opposite
An all-round Champion: *Captain W. Edgeworth-Johnstone, of the Royal Irish*
One of the most popular officers in the Queen's Service is Captain Walter Edgeworth-Johnstone, of the Royal Irish, who for the past twelve months has so capably filled the post of Assistant-Inspector of Gymnasia at Aldershot. He is one of the foremost all-round athletes in the Army. As a boxer, Captain Johnstone is the Amateur Heavy Weight Champion of England, and a holder of the Army Championship and Irish Championship won in Dublin.
As a Sandhurst Cadet, ten years ago, Captain Johnstone captained the R.M.C. Rugby Team, and since then as a Cricketer he has played among the Gentlemen of Ireland, his native country.
Captain Johnstone as a subaltern in his former corps the West India Regiment, has served in three campaigns on the West Coast of Africa. He is a graduate of Trinity College, Dublin, is 33 years of age, stands 6 ft 1 in. in his socks, and scales 13 st 6 lbs.
Before his present appointment he was Superintendent of Gymnasia in the Southern District. Captain Johnstone won the 'Sabre *v.* Sabre' Competition and Challenge Cup at this year's Military Tournament, and also at the recent Army Athletic Meeting at Aldershot.

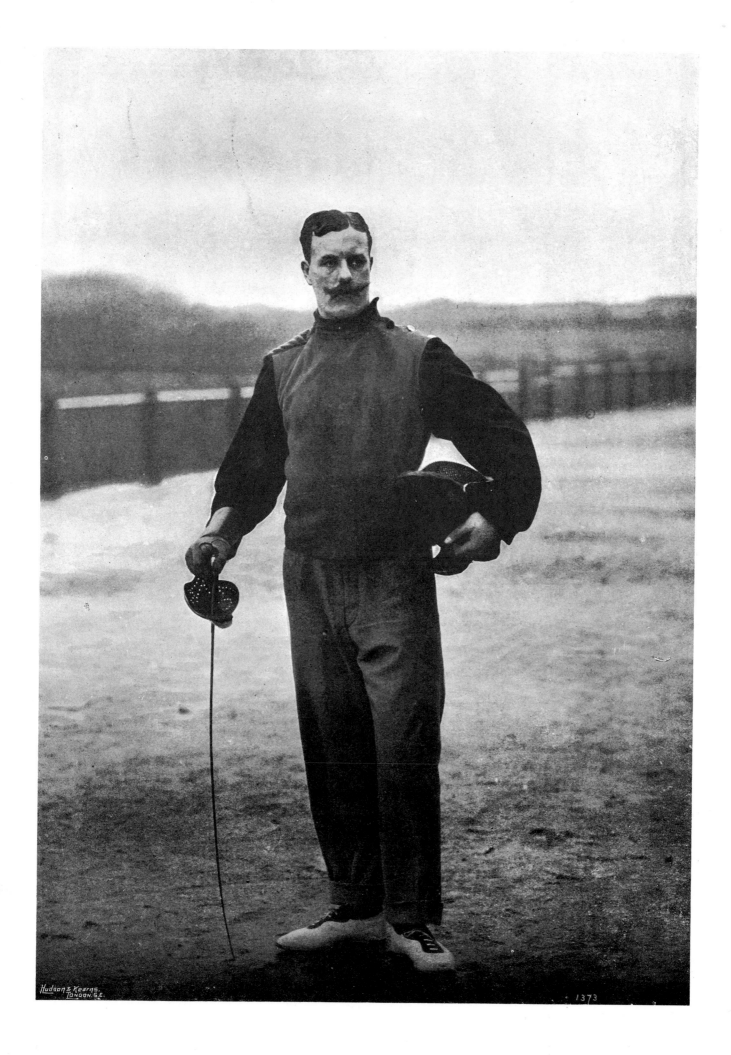

Hudson & Kearns.
London. S.E.

1373

Above

Looking for the 'Enemy'

The above picture represents an outpost of men of the
Warwickshire Regiment practising duty during field manoeuvres
at Malta. The men are admirably ensconced at a point which is
an excellent place of vantage to look out from and watch the
movement of the 'enemy' below. Their service khaki-coloured kit,
blending as it does in colour at any distance with the weathered
stone of the stonework and the ground all round, renders the men
at the same time practically invisible to the 'enemy'.

The caption is an insult to a fine regiment! The fact that three
soldiers are looking away from the enemy, one with his hands
in his pockets looking exceedingly morose, and the one on the
lower right of the picture like a disagreeable bulldog, indicates
that all are waiting for orders before the start of the exercise;
furthermore they resent the presence of the camera, and show it,
little dreaming that the picture will later be published.

Opposite

Our illustration shows Pioneer-Sergeant Stoton, of the 1st Battalion
Grenadier Guards. It has been the custom, from a very long time
back, for Pioneers in the Army to wear beards, if they are able to
grow them, and at the present time, in fact, they are directed to
do so by the Queen's Regulations.

Pioneers were originally destitute peasants who earned a pittance
for the dangerous task of clearing roads in advance of armies.
Although hard and often dangerous, their work has never been
highly esteemed by their comrades.

Hudson & Kearns.

Above

Sons of the 'King's Own'

Many a regiment of Her Majesty's Army can point to certain of its officers and men who have been born and brought up with the colours and are 'Sons of the Regiment' in the fullest sense. Few corps in the Land Service, however, can show so many sons of the regiment of all ranks—both officers and men—as can the 'King's Own', or, as the famous old 4th of the Line, is now officially designated, the 'Royal Lancaster Regiment.' It is a pleasing and interesting picture in every way. Unfortunately, a group such as that we see here must inevitably, in these days of short Service for the rank and file and open competitive examinations for the commisioned officers, tend to become yet more and more rare.

Opposite

In a company barrack room

Here we see the private soldier at home, and obtain a glimpse of barrack-room life by day among the men off duty. Round the room are ranged the men's beds, bedding, and clothes, all neatly and uniformly packed away. On the wall at the head of each bed are placed each man's arms and belts ready at hand at any moment. The men are allowed to decorate the walls of the apartment, each within his allotted space, as they like, with photographs or pictures, and the effect adds greatly to the comfort and appearance of the room. All mess together at the centre table.

As every soldier knows, this is what a barrack room looks like before inspection. Ten minutes later it is a different story. Note the bucket—so highly polished that it could be used as a shaving mirror. Even the pipes—clearly unlit—are at the correct soldierly angle.

THE DOMESTIC LIFE OF TOMMY ATKINS

By G. H. Rayner

It is rather the 'single men in barracks' than their brethren on the 'married strength' into whose private life we propose to venture. There are two men in whose hands lies the principal administrative control of Atkins 'at home'; one is the quartermaster, the other the corporal in charge of Tommy's room. Of course there are intermediate ranks and other parties concerned in looking after the soldier's welfare, but on the quartermaster and corporal the comfort, or otherwise, of the private is chiefly dependent. You will conceive the responsibility on the quartermaster's shoulders when you reflect that he has the housing, provisioning, and clothing of from 600 to 900 men in an infantry regiment, and from 400 to 800 men in a cavalry corps; and, in the latter instance, there are also some 300 to 700 horses whose stabling and forage he is responsible for. It is but bare fact to state that this officer requires intelligence, tact, capacity for work, management, and detail that in civil life would fit him for a high administrative post, and bring him a salary far more adequate than does his military pay. The quartermaster is chosen from the ranks, and his commission is looked upon by the senior non-commissioned officers as a prize always within their reach. The quartermaster arranges the whole of the contracts for provisioning the regiment, and in every possible instance such are placed with local firms. He attends the stores every morning to superintend the weighing of the rations of meat and bread which constitute Government's contribution towards the support of the private soldier. He is responsible for the good quality of these provisions, and the correct allowance for each troop or company. Vegetables, groceries, and the like—which the soldier himself pays for—are all bought from the regimental canteen through the Troop Mess Fund. This fund is managed by the corporals of the troop or company, and every man is put under a certain small weekly stoppage, which goes to the fund. Out of it, potatoes, groceries, beer—on special occasions—and, during winter, extra coal, are bought, and divided in proportion amongst the men. The canteen is managed by a committee of officers, and under the charge of a sergeant, who receives a commission on profits. It is worked on co-operative principles, the profit being annually divided among the troops or companies of the regiment, the divisible amounts being placed to the credit of the different messes.

On joining the headquarters or depôt of his regiment, the soldier is served with a complete outfit. Of this the principal articles are renewed at certain periods, and, with management, they may last the regulation time. But boots, for instance, are apt to wear out sooner than the authorities have calculated, and then Tommy has to provide himself with new ones at his own cost. If any article of his kit be lost, stolen, or strayed, he is also obliged to replace it, and in the case of 'small kit'—under-clothing, brushes, etc.—it can be safely reckoned that some at least of these articles will have to be replaced annually. To make sure a full outfit is always in the possession of each man, ready for active service if necessary, kit inspections are held, on an average, once a month.

Each troop has its regular cook—a man struck off all duty except night guards—and two or more troops occupy one cook-house, under the superintendence of a sergeant-cook.

Every room, which serves the dual purpose of reception and bed room, is under the charge of a corporal, or, occasionally, in the case of a small room, the senior soldier. He is responsible for the cleanliness, order, and discipline of the inmates, and is supposed to see that the men in his charge are duly supplied with their rations, etc. The full strength of the room lend a hand in cleaning it down every morning. Once or twice a week the floor is thoroughly scrubbed down, and on Sunday white-washing and black-leading are rampant: but these duties are the special province of the orderly man. He draws the room's daily rations, and brings up the tea from the cook-house. Breakfast over, he washes up, and then assists in the general clean up of the room. He brings up dinner and tea, and after each meal is responsible for the washing of the crockery and tables. After tea he cleans his mess-tins, and the same having been inspected by the non-commissioned officer in charge of the troop, his duties practically are finished. Once a month, at least, the chief comes round the rooms at dinner-time on a Sunday, and other weeks the troop officers take a tour of inspection; and consequently the room has to be in spick and span order. The floor, forms, and tables are scrubbed to the last scruple of cleanliness; grates and coal-box are black-leaded; walls are white-washed; and every bed and every kit are arranged according to regulation, and in the neatest possible order.

Beer and duff—everyone knows what duff is—are the customary Sunday luxuries, and ultra-refinement, a tablecloth is forthcoming! A knock on the door and a shout of 'shun'. Enter chief, adjutant, quartermaster, and troop officers. The men remain seated, the corporal in charge rising in his place at the head of the table. 'All correct?' asks the colonel. 'All correct, sir,' replies the corporal and exeunt staff, and vanish tablecloth and other vestiges of respectability.

On Sunday afternoon every man not on duty or pleasure bent makes down his bed and goes to sleep. Loud talking or horse-play are dangerous things to attempt in troop-rooms after two p.m. on Sunday. Evenings are devoted to preparation for tomorrow or the canteen, and at 10.15 the fire is made up for the night, and at the sound of the melancholy wailing 'G' that signifies 'lights out', out goes the glim.

If the soldier is unwell, he reports himself 'going sick' first thing after réveille to the orderly sergeant. He is bound to attend early stables or parade; after that he is off duty, until the medical officer has seen him, at any rate. About nine the 'sick call' sounds, and all men for hospital fall in at the guard-room. The sergeant of the guard marches them, along with any prisoners there may be—these latter under escort—to the hospital. There one by one they are examined by the doctor, admitted, put on light duty—outpatients, as it were—or sent back to duty, as the case may be. Any man reporting himself sick without a cause is liable, on detection, to be reported at orderly-room, and his shamming, as a rule, is prescribed for with a stiff dose of drill.

We have now briefly followed the life of Tommy *chez lui*. We might treat of him in hospital, at play, or keeping Christmas; but these phases of his inner life must be kept for another or other articles.

Obeying his Country's call

Typical of what has happened to many a bonny lass is the incident
here depicted, for her lad has to leave her at his country's call.
Perhaps he was a Reservist and the wedding day was already fixed
when the call to arms came. We heartily wish the couple a joyous
reunion.

MILITARY IDIOSYNCRASIES

By 'Drapeau'

Avery long time ago, before the era of scientific education for the mere line officer, and while yet the theory of individual intelligence would have been considered rank heresy, a time when youthful subalterns were not required to possess the culinary knowledge of a *cordon bléu*, and the management of grocery shops and canteens was left to deserving non-commissioned officers in the last year or two of their service, in order that they might thereby attain practical knowledge and sufficient substance to effectually start them in similar lines in civil life – the voice of the man with a predominating idea was occasionally heard in the land. In these days of hard work and practical soldier-ing, in which the 'march past' has ceased to be the be-all and end-all of military training, and the manner of shouldering arms is no longer considered the most thorough test of a regiment's efficiency, in which the practice of the young officer keeping in affectionate proximity to the nearest sergeant when the battalion's movements became a trifle intricate, has almost ceased; the light of the one-idea man is extinguished, his *regime* is numbered with the things that were.

An officer now-a-days, especially a senior officer, has too many irons in the fire to be able to devote undue attention to any particular one, or, verily, he will find himself with burnt fingers.

In the old days things were different. An officer in a high place has been known to get hold of an idea, to tend it and nourish it with loving care till it became his pet and his darling, the very child of his heart, and the juniors steadfastly kept his affection for it in their minds – and were happy.

I remember being inspected by a dear old general, now many years dead. The inspection passed off most satisfactorily, everything met with unqualified approval, and we were congratulating ourselves on the result and the prospective immunity from drill, which then always followed a good inspection when, at the very moment we thought the old gentleman was about to take his departure, his eye sparkled and he turned to the Colonel with a smile on his face. 'I will see your men's pocket-ledgers'. He took up one, turned quickly over that portion of the book wherein is shown the height, chest-measurement, and size of head of the man. Horrors! It hadn't been posted up. Every other one he examined was all right, but that solitary slip was sufficient to blast our reputation in his eyes. And it did.

My memory recalls, from the mists of the past, another inspecting officer who devoted his attention to the condition of the men's boots. Other things might pass, but if one man were found with his boots at all worn at the toes – I don't think he minded the heels so much – the Captain of that man's Company had a bad quarter of an hour. The result was that whatever else was shaky the boots were always in excellent condition, a most essential state of things of course; but in order that there should be no ground for fault-finding, the soles were always built up to an enormous thickness at the toes, and had about as much elasticity as if they had been made of cast-iron.

I remember a rather amusing thing happening in India, in which an Inspecting General, an Irish Medical Officer, and three common house-flies formed the *dramatis personae*.

Early one morning a notification was received that the General purposed inspecting the hospital. Chief among the *bêtes noir* of the distinguished officer in question was a whole-some horror of flies.

Now, every housewife knows the difficulty experienced in getting rid of these little pests during the summer months in England; but in the East they develope a voracity, and attend to business with such persistence, as to leave us nothing but pity for that Egyptian King, who, already sufficiently em-barrassed with the difficulty of keeping the peace between his own working classes and the pauper aliens of the East-ends of Thebes and Memphis, had, in addition, to put up with his clear soup thickened to resemble a furmity pudding, and his Heidsiek's extra sec. like the water in which the pudding-cloths had been washed.

It may therefore be supposed that the intended inspection was the cause of considerable tribulation of mind to the hospital authorities, and most of all to the medical officer in charge.

The hospital was as near perfection as it was possible for a hospital to be; every part of it was spotlessly clean, the grounds were beautifully kept, the patients progressing favourably, and not a single man had any complaint to lay before the general. But how to get rid of the flies, or, at any rate, to manage to get them to absent themselves till after the inspection, was the question that exercised every mind.

The most explicit directions were given to the hospital staff that the whole of their energies were to be devoted to fly fight-ing; but in order to make assurance doubly sure, the Surgeon-Major made a round of the wards and thus addressed the patients:

'Now boys! the gin'ral is coming round, an' he has a howly horror av floies. Oi want ivery mother's son av yez to hunt out every little divil ye see. If there's ne'er a fly whin the gineral comes round oi'll give yez all a bottle av porthor; but, moind oi say; if there's a single one to be seen, its milk diet ye'll be an till further orders.'

Needless to say, every man was on his mettle, and the fly-hunt, as the doctor privately told his *fides achates*, the cantonment magistrate, was 'glorious divarsion'.

Punctual to time came the General and his staff, and he was loud in his praise of everything he saw.

'I must congratulate you, Doctor, on the most excellent con-dition of your hospital. Really I am delighted to see you have managed to get rid of these dreadful pests, the flies. I am always being told that they cannot be entirely got rid of, but I know better, I know better.'

At this moment, he entered the last ward, and the occupants having had to stop the hunt – three flies were buzzing triumphantly round his head.

'Surgeon-Major——! Look at that, Sir! Look at that! There are – one – two – no less than three flies in this ward alone. I must animadvert most strongly on the want of care for the comfort of the patients that the presence of these insects implies.'

'Yez have disgraced me an' yerselves over them flies!' was the refrain of the lecture after the general's departure. 'But sure it wasn't the boy's fault,' he says, in telling the story, 'an' troth! they got their beer in spoite of the gineral's anim-adversions.'

I was told an amusing story once of a Colonel who prided himself, and not without reason, on the smartness of his regiment, but whose knowledge of music was rudimentary. It is the custom, when the band is on parade, to have all instruments of a like description together; the trombones forming one section, the clarionettes another, and so on.

One day the 'Chief' sent for the Band President in great dudgeon. Look here J——' he said, 'I'm not at all satisfied with the Bandmaster. I have complained repeatedly about the way the men are sized, but he is always ready with some cock-and-bull story about keeping the instruments together, really I won't stand it any longer.'

'Shall I send for him Sir' asked the Band President concealing a smile. 'Yes, do; and I'll warn him in your presence.' The Bandmaster came. 'Oh! Mr. Tootler, I've sent to you about the band. I'm not pleased with it.'

'Indeed Sir!' ejaculated the music-master in astonishment, for both he and his band had a high reputation.

'No, I am not, I find you never take the slightest trouble about sizing your men. This morning I saw two small men in the leading section, and just behind them two men very much taller.'

'Yes, Sir, but I must keep the instruments together.' 'Of course, you must keep the instruments together, Sir; but you must change the men about. If a man is too small for the trombones you must put him in the clarionette ranks, and *vice versa*.' Those who understand a Bandmaster's pride in his specialists, and the technicality called 'lip' will appreciate the situation.

Sometimes an officer has been known to draw upon himself an unenviable reputation as a faddist, for no other reason than because his ideas were a little in advance of the times.

Such a case occurred in a certain cavalry regiment, distinguished alike for its service in the field, its conduct in quarters, and its smartness at all times. The Captain of, shall we say 'M' troop—for in those days squadrons were not—was an exceedingly capable officer, and carried his ideas of thoroughness to an extent exasperating to his subaltern, who was in constant hot water over his failure to grasp the importance of numerous items of interior economy which his chief was always inculcating. 'Mr. Smith,' the latter would say, 'you must really try to realize how essential it is to be thoroughly conversant with everything concerning the men and horses; you should be able to say at once what a man's character is, his age, his occupation before he enlisted, and, in short, everything about him.'

Well, Smith having procured a note-book, by dint of much questioning and searching of documents managed to obtain a more or less correct *précis* of the personal history of the men of the troop, which he furtively studied when he could manage to elude the vigilance of his brother subs.; and, so far as the men were concerned, got on fairly well. With the horses, however, he was completely at sea, and dreaded the inevitable catechizing at stables accordingly. Never could he tell one animal from another.

'What horse is this?' the Captain would say pleasantly.

'Really, I'm afraid—that is—I—er don't think I remember his number.' 'Very well. What one is this?'

Poor Smith would look as if he knew all about it, suddenly find that he didn't, and then gaze all round the stable for inspiration, the troop sergeant-major looking straight to his front with the face of a sphinx. Smith was unhappy, for, of course, his brother subs. by no means permitted him to forget his weak point; and to have the query, 'What horse is this, Smith?' whispered in his ear amidst the entrancing bliss of a waltz with a pretty girl, was, to say the least, disconcerting. He was determined to put a stop to it. But how? He thought over the matter for many nights and at last hit on a scheme. In order to carry it into effect, however, it was necessary to take the troop sergeant-major into his confidence. What transpired between Smith and that astute non-commissioned officer deponent knoweth not; but next day at stables, when the Captain trotted out his usual question, 'What horse is this, Mr. Smith?' like a flash came the reply, '23, sir;' the next

question and the next being answered with equal readiness. But that captain was no fool. A day or two afterwards he again went round the stables, Smith as usual, following him up, the sergeant-major with his inscrutable face immediately behind.

The skipper was in a particularly good humour, and was chatting most amicably, apparently taking little notice of anything. Suddenly, in a good natured off-hand way, laying his hand on a horse's croup, he asked: *What* horse is this, Smith?'

A furtive glance to the corner of the stall followed the question, and the reply came promptly.

'Oh! that's number 37.'

'Lead it out,' said the Captain to one of the men. The horse was turned so that the light fell on his fore-feet.

'I'm afraid you've made a mistake,' said the Captain raising his eye-brows slightly. 'However, we'll try another.' Another was tried, with no better success. Poor Smith looked sheepish. Nothing more was said until they left the stables. Then the Captain stopped and turned to him with a smile.

'Look here, Smith,' he remarked quietly, 'the next time you want to recognize a horse by having his number chalked up on his stall, you had better make sure that he won't be changed to another one.'

Smith is in the Infantry now.

THE OLD SOLDIER

By Callum Beg

'Where are the boys of the Old Brigade?' asks the well-known military song. We cannot undertake to give a satisfactory answer; but wherever the heroes may be, there cannot be more difficulty in discovering their whereabouts than there is at the present day in unearthing an old soldier proper.

We use the word *proper* advisedly, not in its heraldic sense (for that means *au naturel*, and consequently in most instances *im*proper), but because there are those who, without having proved their title to the style, are known as 'old soldiers'. This is the fault of no one in particular, but merely of the short-service system which has fixed seven years as the recognized term of military service. What wonder, then, that in a Line battalion a man of over five years' service should be held a veteran. Suffice it, in this connection, to say that these young soldiers, however deserving they may be of notice, will not enter into this article. We are concerned rather with a bygone type, a species that is well-nigh extinct. The class of man with whom we intend to deal is seldom found on parade. If he forms a part of a regiment or corps, it is not in the drill-ground that the old soldier is to be sought. No doubt the uncharitable would at once use this as an argument in favour of short service. 'He is not found on parade,' they would say, 'because his old bones are incapable of bearing arms'; but softly, O uncharitable one! The old soldier has a young heart withal. Nor is it because he is unfit for duty that he is invisible on parade. As a matter of fact, he is a man of too much value in barracks to be 'warned' for adjutant's parade. More interesting work has been found for him than the continual forming of half-company and sectional columns on the march, thereby materially assisting in crushing the gravel on the regimental parade ground.

Where then is the worthy to be met with, and how does he employ his time? First, we may see him face to face in the regimental shoemakers' or tailors' shop. Here he appears to great advantage, for there is nothing to prevent his conversing freely while he plies his awl or makes some important repairs in a kersey frock (value 3s. 8d.), his legs crossed in the orthodox manner. He is a good conversationalist, and the old soldier and his yarns are interesting, provided one has not heard them on a former occasion. Inspiriting stories they are, in which are mixed, with due regard to effect, battles, murders, and sudden deaths from fever, cholera, or an encounter hand-to-hand with a man-eating tiger. The listener, indeed, is puzzled to know how the yarn-spinner, the eye-witness of so many horrible sights, escaped alive.

At times he occupies the position of officer's servant, and here he is at his best. How well he darns the young officer's stockings; how carefully he folds his clothes; how regularly he calls him in time for parade, and warns him for duty; how firmly he reprimands him in the morning if he has exceeded the bounds on a guest night; how quietly, in fine, does he help himself to his master's 'Buchanan' if he is feeling 'weakly'.

It may be that he is a waiter in the canteen, a clerk in the orderly-room or quartermaster's stores, or orderly to his commanding officer. In whatever way he may be employed he furnishes ample study for the archaeologist.

If a married man, he is usually a dutiful husband, and one meets him in town every Saturday evening, arm-in-arm with the 'old girl' – the latter carrying a basket. If, however, he has not entered the holy estate, he is invaluable in the barrack-room. Accustomed to discipline, he is well qualified to keep the room in order in the absence of the non-commissioned officer. In fact, the old soldier regards his barrack-room as being among his 'regimental necessaries', and the recruit who is careless enough to enter with muddy boots, or to upset his soup on the floor, would ten times rather come before the commanding officer for punishment than before Private Bronzeface, whose awards are more of a summary nature than those sanctioned by Queen's Regulations. Our old friend is usually a man of good character, though he is not averse to the 'flowing bowl', but he has one great fault. It has become so much a part of himself, however, that we have ceased to regard it as such.

He grumbles with marked regularity. If the dinner is not under-done, he pronounces it over-cooked. If the sun shines, it is too hot for marching. If it rains, he 'growls' because his straps are soiled. If a parade is ordered at 5.30, it is too early; if at 10.30, it is too late. But, for all his grumbling, the old soldier will never permit a 'youngster' to complain. Such insolence the veteran would at once suppress. Sad it is that such a venerable type should be all but extinct. Yes, old soldier, 'with all thy faults, we love thee still'.

Hudson & Kearns,
London, S.E.

105

THE COLONIES

By the close of the nineteenth century the British empire was at its height, incomparably greater than any other, comprising some four hundred million people. During the last fifteen years of the century the process of expansion had been accelerated by the acquisition of vast territories in Africa; and it was the British determination to keep a grip on Southern Africa which in 1899 led to the Boer War.

At the heart of the empire, however, was India, with its population of over three hundred million, one sixth of the human race.

Nevertheless, the innate British sense of superiority, and of our god-given duty to subdue and govern, was not completely secure. It had been given a nasty jolt in 1857 during the Indian Mutiny. Moreover, the strains of administering an empire of this size—Britain's population was a mere forty million and there was no conscript army—were beginning to take their toll as the new century began.

A Frontier outpost

Inside a Frontier fort

A home from home

'Whether or not there is going to be more trouble with the tribes on the Punjab frontier remains to be seen. One thing, however, is certain, that if there is we mean to be ready for it.'

Part of our 'readiness' was the Barah fort, headquarters of the Tirah Field Force.

Above
'Al-fresco' – *Royal Niger Haussas at dinner.*

In spite of the difficulties caused by other countries, mainly France and Germany, trying to make treaties with chiefs who were already bound to us, we were doing reasonably well in Africa. However, 'It is not proposed to give long strings of heathen names, which are spelt differently in every atlas, except where they are altogether omitted, it is sufficient to point out that by virtue of treaties and arrangements, dating back in some instances twelve years, we have acquired rights in certain localities. Can a Frenchman say the same?' As some of the local chiefs seemed neither to know nor to care who they were signing treaties with – and the territorial boundaries of Germany, France, Italy, etc. cannot have been all that clear, we organized local colonial troops who would have no doubts about whose side they were on. These are from northern Nigeria.

Left
Non-Commissioned Officers and Private, Royal Niger Haussas

Opposite, top
Officer and detachment, 2nd West India Regiment

Opposite, bottom
Officer, non-commissioned officer, and detachment, Sierra Leone frontier force

Field Service Kit—front view

Field Service Kit—back view

The 'campaigning kit' has the white webbing well blancoed; this would later be replaced by khaki, as a result of costly experience in casualties.

Royal Canadian Dragoon sentry in winter uniform

Canada, which had been a self-governing Dominion since 1867, is
still listed in these pages as a 'colony'.

The Halifax Artillery in winter dress. No wonder cricket never
became popular in Canada!

A Depot recruiting party, W.I.R.

Encouraging men to 'follow the drum'.

Chinese in British Army service

Life in a Burma Regiment

The pictures on this and the opposite page are of a regiment on active service, when mistakes meant death and disaster. The picture above shows the heliograph, capable of signalling over 90 miles in silence and secrecy. The top picture shows the essential supervision needed to prevent fiddling with the rations. The top picture on the opposite page shows rifle practice, and the picture below it shows the guard over prisoners in the stocks—unguarded, they would have made a speedy escape.

Christmas in Burma

Christmas in the Hills

Absence from our native land makes all the old Christmas customs doubly dear to us, and the day is on that account more royally kept in India than at home. There is, in addition, all the pleasure of looking forward to the incoming mail bringing with it presents and cards from friends in England. In fact, the arrival by post of a plum pudding is not an unheard of event. Such has often been the welcome 'Christmas-box' of some fond mother's son wearing Her Majesty's uniform in the East. On one occasion at least, the recipient had the satisfaction of beholding it carried in solemn procession, shoulder high, before being placed for consumption on his barrack-room table. As well as the orthodox modes of spending Christmas, the climate in most parts of India admits of further enjoyment, rendered impracticable in England by frost, snow, or cold. In the first photograph we see British officers and their friends in Burma, listening to the band in the cool of the evening. The second represents one of those picnic gatherings in the neighbourhood of a Hill Station—a social function, which is the outcome of hospitality, almost unknown at home. It forms a pleasant prelude to a sumptuous Christmas dinner, at which those at home are heartily toasted.

The British officers seem to take their music lying down—or is it the effect of tinned Christmas pudding?

Major-General Sir C. Holled Smith,
Commandant of the Victorian Forces

Rissaldar Gurdath Singh,
12th Bengal Cavalry, and Orderly.

A Rissaldar commanded a half-squadron.

A heavy battery of the Indian Army on parade
The Indian Army has on its establishment four 'Heavy Batteries',
as they are called – each battery being made up of four 40-pdrs and
two 6.3 inch howitzers – recently re-distributed, two in the Punjab,
one in Bengal, and one in Madras. Each battery, as far as the guns
are concerned, is manned entirely by Royal Artillerymen (of the
Garrison Companies), the normal strength of these being, one major
(in command), one captain, three subalterns, two staff-sergeants, six
corporals, six bombardiers, and seventy-two gunners, with two
trumpeters and one farrier. There are twelve elephants to each
battery, two to a gun or howitzer, with, to look after them – one
jemader, twelve Mahouts, and twelve assistant Mahouts.

For transport 262 bullocks are attached to the battery managed
by – one jemadar, six sirdars, and 131 drivers. The total strength in
men of all ranks, European and native, in a Heavy Battery is 163.
The European officers are, of course, mounted as usual. Our
photograph shows a Heavy Battery on parade, with the European
detachment to each 'division', or pair of guns, at the head of the
'division', drawn up in front of the guns.

The motto of the Royal Artillery is 'Quo fas et gloria ducunt'
(Where right and glory lead). Elephants can be impulsive and
evil-tempered and those standing in front may well have
felt – though they would never show – apprehension.

The Victoria Forces possess and practise with a muzzle-loader.

The Sergeant-Major and the Regimental pet, Victorian
Mounted Rifles

A Regimental pet—Australian style.

In 1895 the Prince of Chitral, on the North West frontier of India, was murdered; his killer then proceeded to besiege the small British forces in Chitral. A relief expedition under Colonel Kelly eventually relieved the beleaguered garrison. Its approach was made extremely difficult by the wild and rugged nature of the country it had to traverse. These pictures are of Maxim guns being transported on mules and subsequently being handled by the King's Own Scottish Borderers and the Devonshire Regiment. The two bridges are examples of Royal Engineers bridging. Each was built in less than 48 hours.

WARS IN THE SUDAN

Between 1881 and 1885, and again between 1896 and 1898, we were engaged in two wars in the Sudan. In the first phase our half-hearted efforts were defeated by the Mahdi and his Dervish army, and the war ended with the murder in Khartoum of General Gordon, who is pictured above.

Soon afterwards the Mahdi died and his place was taken by the Khalifa. The British Government had no wish to be involved in expensive conflicts in the Soudan and made no further efforts. However, by 1896 it was obvious that the Khalifa had established a considerable tyranny and that if we did not intervene one of our imperial rivals—probably the French—would step in and establish colonial rule. Command of a reconquest expedition was given to Kitchener, then 'Sirdar' (i.e. Commander-in-Chief) of the Egyptian army. Reconquest was largely a matter of logistics. Nile gunboats were organized and a railway was built. There was a fierce battle at Atbara and a larger one at Omdurman. The latter was notable for the courage of the Dervishes and the brave but culpably reckless charge of the 21st Lancers, who were launched over unknown and hazardous ground.

Photo. by G. Lekegian & Co.
KITCHENER OF KHARTOUM.

Warriors of the Nile
A Souvenir of Omdurman and Khartoum

Kitchener was 49 at the time of this picture.

Above and left
The open air service is being held at the Kasr-el-Nil Barracks, Cairo for the 2nd Rifle Brigade and 2nd Lancashire Fusiliers. 'Both are splendid bodies of men and will undoubtedly fight even better than they can pray,' says the accompanying caption.
 The two colour-sergeants, one standing at attention and the other at ease, are both in the Rifle Brigade. They are fully protected against the sun. The 'helmet curtain' on their topees shades the neck and a 'spine protector' prevents a man getting sunstroke through the spine.
 Nowadays, when the term 'sunstroke' has been replaced by 'heatstroke', this elaborate garb may seem more of a hindrance than a help, but many people still prefer to have some sort of shade, even if they have to wear it.

Opposite
The 'Camerons' on the march

The Camerons can scarcely be described as 'on the march' as the original caption says. They have halted, and have piled arms. 'Piled' arms were usually arranged in threes so that they could be snatched up at a moment's notice.

A wood-cutting party

A call to arms

Returning from church

Ready

After the first Attack

Resting after the battle

General Gatacre

Some Dervish prisoners

Awaiting the Dervish attack

These pictures were taken before, during and after the Battle of Omdurman. General Gatacre added to his laurels; here he is not as public relations minded as a modern general would be.

The Camel Corps practising square formation is a very small example of what was usually a much larger and vital manoeuvre against surprise attack.

Some leaders in the famous charge at Omdurman

The officers of the 21st Lancers

The sergeants of the 21st Lancers

The 21st Lancers, the youngest of the Lancer regiments, achieved fame at Omdurman in a charge which went wrong. A depression in the ground concealed large numbers of waiting Dervishes. The 21st fought with tremendous courage and dash. Five officers and two sergeants were killed, two officers and four sergeants were wounded.

THE SOUTH AFRICAN WAR

It may be, and no doubt it is, a proof of spirit in corps of Volunteers to offer to serve against the Boers; but does not all this zeal trench a little on the absurd? One finds some difficulty in seeing anything magnanimous in the simultaneous efforts of 40,000,000 to deal with 25,000. But apart from considerations of that kind, and from the question of taste, is it not the case that corps of Volunteers which offer to serve over sea are going against the very principle by which they exist? That individual Volunteers should enter the ranks of the Army is one thing, but that corps of them should go out of the British Isles is another. The theory concerning the Volunteers is that they are to stand by to replace the regular soldiers who are sent abroad, so that the country shall not be left without an armed and organized garrison in case an enemy should contrive to slip through the British Fleet and invade us. How that feat could be achieved and whether it ever will be achieved, are pretty subjects for debate; but it is the fact that the whole organization of the Volunteers is for home services, and will be reduced to nonsense if they are to be sent abroad.

'Good-bye, Daddy, wish I was going too'
'The above pictured incident is only one of hundreds of a similar
nature which have taken place in the past few days. The boy
knows nothing of grim war, but is fascinated by the idea of a
journey in a big "steamboat". It is to be hoped he will welcome
his father home again.'

Never mind, sonny, you'll get your chance in 1914–18.

The South African War (often called the Boer War – the Dutch/ Afrikaans word for farmer was 'Boer') was the result of long-standing rivalry. The Cape of Good Hope had been colonized by the Dutch, but after 1814 the British acquired it by purchase. When Britain abolished slavery in 1834, the Dutch settlers decided that their overlords were mad, and tried to get away from them for ever by uprooting themselves and moving northward on the Great Trek.

Eventually the Boers were granted two independent states. However, diamonds and gold in huge quantities were soon discovered in Boer territory. The Boers lost control of the diamonds but were determined to retain control of the gold deposits at all costs. Foreigners, who included British, were denied the most basic rights in the Transvaal. A half-hearted effort to assert themselves by the British in 1881 had been ignominiously defeated by the Boers who, in consequence, treated further British protests and threats with contempt.

By 1899 all attempts at reconciliation had failed. Paul Kruger, the Boer leader, who in his youth had been on the Great Trek, distrusted the British and would not give an inch. Heavy purchases of arms by the Boers led to a British ultimatum. As a result the Boers began the war by invading British territory. Soon they were winning dramatic victories and besieging Ladysmith, Mafeking and Kimberley. The height of disaster was reached in 'Black Week' in December 1899, when the British sustained major defeats at Stormberg, Magersfontein and Colenso. The fact that the Boers were brilliant guerrilla fighters, and that they were campaigning in an area as large as the combined size of France and Germany, put the problems beyond the intellectual reach of the initial commanders, who were already hampered by inadequate backing from home. What had been thought to be not much more than a matter of teaching a few stupid farmers a sharp lesson turned out to be a war in which the 'farmers' mustered 90,000 men, fought with unexpected skill, used modern equipment, such as smokeless powder, and made the best possible use of rugged territory.

The tide turned when Lord Roberts (Bobs) took over as Commander-in-Chief in February 1900. By November of the same year, Roberts had transformed humiliating defeat into the certainty of victory. Nevertheless, it was left to his successor, Lord Kitchener, the 'hero of Omdurman', to crush guerrilla resistance and to consolidate victory. In reality, Kitchener was no hero and no great field commander, but he was intelligent, patient and methodical, and this was the formula required to defeat the Boers, even though the process took a further eighteen months.

The Boers gave the British army some sharp lessons, and this led to a number of reforms. Unfortunately, some of the deductions made in the Boer War led to dangerous assumptions at the beginning of World War I.

For Soldiers' and Sailors' Kith and Kin
Prominent workers for the cause

Unfortunately no details of their work 'For Pity's Sake' are recorded.

Above

The war had just begun. The nurses were on their way out with no concept of what they would encounter; the troops, as usual, thought the war would be over by Christmas; and the cavalry were sharpening swords, with which they would doubtless cut down Boer marksmen. It looked like being a comfortable little war.

But, as a correspondent said, 'We are not entering the struggle under any illusions. We have known all along that this is to be no kid glove business whether the fighting lasts six weeks or six months.' What he was saying two years later is not recorded.

Opposite

Off for South Africa

The orders detailing the troops which are to proceed to the front have divided the Army into two parties—those who regret they cannot go and those who are delighted at having been selected. The former wish 'God-speed' to the latter, though they cannot help envying them their good fortune.

But, of course, it was quite fair. Almost everyone got a turn eventually.

Wire entanglements on the Tugela.
Some of the obstacles encountered by our troops.

The shape of things to come.

Sharpening penknives, and painting scabbards khaki colour to
prevent the sun-glint.

This was war. Scabbards must be painted not polished.

The observation balloon at Ladysmith.

Our Special Correspondent who was locked up in Ladysmith sends
us an illustration of the balloon being sent up to observe the Boer
positions. He writes that 'this balloon has been a source of great
annoyance to the Boers.'

But not enough to make them lift the siege, unfortunately.

On the Orange River Frontier

A typical South African kopjes—a position near Colesberg. The above gives a most excellent idea of one of those kopjes of which we now hear so much, and is one of those occupied by our troops near Colesberg. The officer in the centre is Colonel Porter, who commands the 6th Dragoon Guards, better known as the Carabiniers. The colonel and his regiment are now with French pushing on to Bloemfontein, and the former commands one of that general's brigades which did sterling work in the recent operations.

The Eyes and Ears of the Press.
Special Correspondents watching the fight.

A 4.7 in. in action.
The Bluejackets clear the enemy out of Fort Wylie.

The Red Cross in action.
Bringing up the Ambulance Waggon.

Ambulance Parties at work.
The R.A.M.C. bringing in wounded.

With Hildyard's Brigade.
Some of the Supports taking cover.

Sir Redvers Buller and a War Correspondent

From the intent attitude of Mr. Bennett Burleigh, who is now at the front in Natal, he would appear to be receiving from the General some information of special interest. We may be quite sure, however, that the knowledge will not be sent home so as to be in any way useful to our friend the enemy. The experienced correspondent knows his work too well for that, and the Press Censor lurks behind.

Burleigh and the General were old friends. Burleigh, a most experienced correspondent, was probably able to tell the General more than he knew himself.

The Heroes we Mourn.

A picture of the first casualties. They included a General and a full Colonel.

ACKNOWLEDGMENTS

The illustrations which appear
in this book are taken from
NAVY AND ARMY ILLUSTRATED,
first published in 1895 by
Hudson & Kearns, and George Newnes Ltd.,
with the exception of the following:

Hamlyn Group Picture Library:
Page 132.

National Army Museum:
Pages 6–7, 106.

Radio Times Hulton Picture Library:
Pages 124, 134.